THE POETRY CORNER

Other books and materials by Arnold B. Cheyney and Jeanne S. Cheyney

TEACHING CHILDREN OF DIFFERENT CULTURES IN THE CLASSROOM: A Language Approach
THE RIPE HARVEST: Educating Migrant Children (editor)
TEACHING READING SKILLS THROUGH THE NEWSPAPER
THE PUPPET ENRICHMENT PROGRAM (with Georgia B. Adams)
PRESS: A Handbook Showing the Use of Newspapers in the Elementary Classroom
VIDEO: A Handbook Showing the Use of the Television in the Elementary Classroom
(with Rosemary Lee Potter)
THE WRITING CORNER
THE SECRET OF GILTHAM HALL (an adult novel by Jeanne S. Cheyney)

THE POETRY CORNER

Scott, Foresman and Company

Glenview, IL   London, England

THE POETRY CORNER

Arnold B. Cheyney
University of Miami

Illustrated by Jeanne S. Cheyney
University of Miami

ISBN 0-673-16461-6

Printed in the United States of America.

9101112131415 – BKC – 92

CONTENTS

Appendix 61

PREFACE

The Poetry Corner is designed for teachers who want to teach children to write poetically. Perhaps some will become poets, but that is not the intent of this writing. It is my hope that children will gain some understanding and skill in poetic language and find enjoyment in poetry.

The book takes readers into the past of poetry through a broad selection of poets and their works. Some of the poems of the past have gone the way of all language; they have changed. The phrases you remember and the way you repeated them may be different from the ones in this volume. There is a truth here that should not escape us. Poetry changes and expands in style and form just as the disciplines of music and art. An unfamiliar form of poetry may seem incongruous to a reader when in poetic terms it is just another aspect of language change. It's good to cherish the old for there are the roots, the foundations, for building the new.

What is *The Poetry Corner* about? It's about encouraging children to play and create with language. It's using children's experiences, their present levels of development, and their present levels of interests as a means to explore poetic language. It's learning to think, feel, and be at home in a poetic world.

The Poetry Corner will help you explore and evoke the poetic language of children. It will give you practical ways of developing language preciseness with children. Finally, it will outline procedures for sharing these experiences in oral and written forms.

Many students and teachers in my classes and workshops have served as sources of encouragement by using the poetic devices in this book successfully. I am indebted to them.

May I suggest that you find a secluded spot, leisurely thumb through the pages, and try to write your own poems. Then, enthusiastically share your writing and these poetic activities with children.

Arnold B. Cheyney

INTRODUCTION

The central purpose of *The Poetry Corner* is to encourage children through their teachers to "fool around" with poetic writing free from the constraints of meter and rhyme. Most children will no more become poets in the traditional sense than children become artists by having art classes once a week. In the same vein, few children become accomplished musicians by having a music teacher visit a classroom on an occasional basis. While possibilities exist for becoming artists and musicians, so do possibilities exist for children to become poets; hence some discussion and activities for meter and rhyme are found here.

A distinction is made between poetry and poetic writing. The great mass of writing done by children and dubbed "poetry" is not actually poetry from the author's point of view.* While poetry is difficult to define and set within parameters, general agreement or consensus is generally found among poets and students of poetry on what poetry is not. The doggerel and early poetic musing of children is at least distinguishable to many.

The term "poetic writing" is found quite often in this book. It indicates the expectation that children will begin writing with an eye toward the poetic. It is hoped many will relish and find excitement in poetic language. Perhaps they will experience a dimension in this area of the arts that will pull them into the joys of poetry throughout their lives. The Czech biologist and poet, Miroslav Holub, saw poetry as part of the average person's normal life pattern: "I would like them to read poems as naturally as they read the papers, or go to a football game."

Although *The Poetry Corner* is not an anthology, it contains poems and references to poetry of the last several centuries. By listening to and reading poetry (poems that are generally agreed upon as poems through the test of continued use and popularity) perhaps some children can expand their vision of poetry and its usefulness in their lives.

The rhythm, cadence, and meter that masters of poetry contributed to this genre of literature should not be lost. The taste of

*See Myra Cohn Livingston, "But Is It Poetry," *The Horn Book Magazine*, Part I, December 1975, pp. 571-580; Part II, February 1976, pp. 24-31.

the best of past years and present years gives children standards of quality with which to make judgments of their own work.

Of the many ways of touching the poetic psyches of children, two are essential. First, children must hear poetry read aloud. This, of course, implies that the reader knows how to select poetry for reading aloud and enjoys sharing poetry in this way. Second, children must have the opportunity to involve themselves in the mind stretching language exercise of putting pen to paper and creating.

Children are more comfortable with restraints than with unsupervised freedom. This is true not only in the behavioral areas but also the academic. Formula type poetic exercise loosens literary creativity within structure. The syllabic and word poetic writing found in this book help children focus their language skills. The forms are short enough that children are not overwhelmed by the task. Therefore, experience shows they write much more than required. Rhyming is not necessary in these types of poetic writings so there are no gaps to be plugged in by finding the right rhyming fit.

These structures are meant as starting places. Expect to bend, expand, dismantle, and eventually ignore them as the inner voices of children find their way into poetic expression.

CHAPTER 1

Who wants to understand the poem
Must go to the land of poetry;
Who wishes to understand the poet
Must go to the poet's land.

Johann Wolfgang Von Goethe (1749–1832)

EXPLORING THE POET'S LAND

Poetry draws from inside us images which are flashed on the screens of our minds. Colorful pictures twist by. Insights swirl within us, dart to the outer limits of our space, perhaps to return, perhaps not.

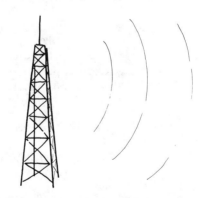

THE POETIC WORLD

We live in the world of the poetic—
optical
    illusory
        bewitching.
    Poetry travels on
radio waves
    television signals
We chatter alliteratively— "What a stupendous sale at Sears!"
Our speech becomes accidentally poetic at the supermarket:

The lettuce is so green.
So are the beans.
Hey, that rhymes!
Why, we're poets.
And didn't even know it.

Ever happen to you? Poetry surrounds us. On the playground as nursery rhymes are chanted:

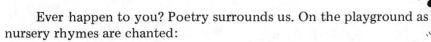

Jack be nimble,
Jack be quick,
Jack, jump over the candle stick.

On tombstones in long forgotten cemeteries, epitaphs wearily maintain their vigils:

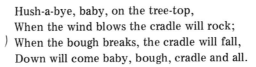

> A zealous locksmith died of late,
> And did arrive at heaven gate,
> He stood without and would not knock,
> Because he meant to pick the lock.

In our music, when we comfort the young:

> Hush-a-bye, baby, on the tree-top,
> When the wind blows the cradle will rock;
> When the bough breaks, the cradle will fall,
> Down will come baby, bough, cradle and all.

In our music, as comfort for the not so young:

> We shall overcome, we shall overcome,
> We shall overcome some day.*

Poetry tickles us in the nursery:

> This little pig went to market;
> This little pig stayed home;
> This little pig had roast beef;
> This little pig had none;
> And this little pig cried, Wee, wee, wee!
> All the way home.

and

> Pat-a-cake, pat-a-cake, baker's man
> Bake me a cake as fast as you can;
> Pat it and prick it, and mark it with a B,
> Put it in the oven for baby and me.

Often poetry is not recognized. Consider the parallelism in Isaiah:

> All we like sheep have gone astray;
> We have turned everyone to his own way;

Or that of the Proverbs:

> The glory of young men is their strength:
> and the beauty of old men is the gray head.

WHAT IS POETRY?

Definitions are many but none are all encompassing. Who can say, "This is a poem; that is not."

*"We Shall Overcome" was originally sung on slave plantations before the Civil War. At the turn of the century it became a formal Baptist hymn. Black workers used it as a protest theme in 1946 on picket lines in Charleston, South Carolina.

Democritus, dead some 2,400 years, said rather pointedly to those concerned with poetry:

> Whatever a poet writes
> with enthusiasm and a divine inspiration
> is very fine.

Poetry is as diverse as individual poets. Definitions range from the simple—"Poetry is words put together that give me happiness—" to the didactic—"Poetry is a form of literature written in rhyme and meter—" to the flippant—"What is poetry? Why, that's what poets write."

Take your pick, or make up your own.

The purists in the land of poetry cringe when writers explore new arrangements such as scrambling typeface letters on 20 pound bond paper, calling the confusion *poetry*.

To them poetry must *look* like poetry. Poetry must trip along the tongue. The best poetry rhymes, they say.

Here is one of the best by all standards. Read it aloud. If someone is in the room with you and you are embarrassed, find a place to hide yourself away. Or get up your courage and read part of William Blake's (1757–1827) "The Songs of Innocence" to them.

Piping down the valleys wild,
Piping songs of pleasant glee,
On a cloud I saw a child,
And he laughing said to me:

"Pipe a song about a Lamb!"
So I piped with merry cheer.
"Piper, pipe that song again;"
So I piped, he wept to hear.

"Drop thy pipe, thy happy pipe;
Sing thy songs of happy cheer:"
So I sung the same again,
While he wept with joy to hear.

"Piper, sit thee down and write
In a book that all may read."
So he vanish'd from my sight,
And I pluck'd a hollow reed,

And I made a rural pen,
And I stain'd the water clear,
And I wrote my happy songs
Every child may joy to hear.

What, then, is poetry? Many things.

Poetry is a grinning boy mischievously creating satire in a comic book format: *Mad Magazine*.

Poetry is an electronic Mork playing word games in our living rooms with Mindy.

Poetry is children on the sidewalk singing

Jumping Jack, Jumping Jack,
Missed a crack and broke his back.

Poetry is singing "The Star Spangled Banner" before a football game on a crisp, fall Saturday afternoon.

Poetry is the Pledge of Allegiance being said in a one-room schoolhouse in the midwest:

I pledge allegiance
to the flag of the United States of America
and
to the Republic for which it stands,
one nation under God,
indivisible,
with liberty and justice
for all.

Poetry is Robert Frost writing "and miles to go before I sleep" or a voice entreating, "Grandpa, read my poem."

Poetry is singing an ABC song:

A B C D
E F G
H I J K
L M N O P
Q R S
T U V
W X Y Z
Now I know my A B C's,
Tell me what you think of me.

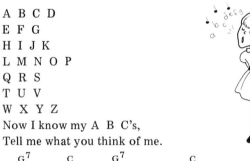

Poetry is Ludwig Bemelmans creating *Madeline* in a children's book and writing the text in poetry. Madeline promptly goes rhymingly off to the hospital to have her appendix removed.

After all the poets, would-be poets, and learned men and women have had their say, it is Eleanor Farjeon explaining ever so adroitly:

What is Poetry? Who knows?
Not a rose, but the scent of the rose;
Not the sky, but the light in the sky;
Not the fly, but the gleam of the fly;
Not the sea, but the sound of the sea;
Not myself, but what makes me
See, hear, and feel something that prose
Cannot: and what it is, who knows?*

And what it is, who knows?

*"Poetry" from *Eleanor Farjeon's Poems for Children*. Originally published in *Sing for Your Supper* by Eleanor Farjeon. Copyright 1938 by Eleanor Farjeon. Renewed 1966 by Gervase Farjeon. Reprinted by permission of J. B. Lippincott, Publishers.

CHAPTER 2

The proper and immediate object
of poetry is the communication
of immediate pleasure.

Samuel Taylor Coleridge (1772–1834)

EVOKING POETIC WRITING

Not everybody can be a poet. Not everybody wants to be one. Some who do, do so for the wrong reasons. In Ciardi's *How Does a Poem Mean?** "W. H. Auden was once asked what advice he would give a young man who wished to become a poet. Auden replied that he would ask the young man why he wanted to write poetry. If the answer was 'because I have something important to say,' Auden would conclude that there was no hope for that young man as a poet. If on the other hand the answer was something like 'because I like to hang around words and overhear them talking to one another,' then that young man was at least interested in a fundamental part of the poetic process and there was hope for him."

THE LOGOPHILE

The word logophile aptly describes a person who enjoys "hanging around words." *Logo* and *phile* have Greek roots roughly translatable to mean "word lover." Encouraging children to be word lovers is at the heart of poetic communication. One primary teacher cut half-inch strips of construction paper, printed "logophile" on each one plus a new vocabulary word, then attached them as bands to her children's wrists. The proud parents were quick to point out to friends and relatives that *their* children were learning Greek in school!

*John Ciardi and Miller Williams, *How Does a Poem Mean?* 2nd ed. (Boston: Houghton Mifflin, 1975), p. 3.

TALKING

An editorial in *The Hartford Courant* of August 24, 1897 stated, "Everybody talks about the weather, but nobody does anything about it." The weather is the favorite opening line of conversation between friends or strangers. It is also a major theme among poets.

Nature responds to weather with the bleak trees of winter, the new green of spring, and the colorful leaves of autumn. Children respond to a discussion of weather through expanding vocabulary. The chalkboard divided into seasons—summer, autumn, winter, spring—evokes listings of words for later use in poetic writing. Here is a start:

Summer	*Autumn*	*Winter*	*Spring*
humid	leaves	icicles	lush
hot	golden	snow	green
sweat	bronze	swirl	cool
dog days	red	slush	grass

As children enter the classroom after being jostled by the cold winds and snow of a winter morning, with their cheeks still smarting and their fingers tingling, try writing down their comments about how they feel, what they saw, what they heard. Ask them: What did the wind do? What did the snow feel like? What sounds did you hear? Then have them paint pictures of the morning with words.

INDIVIDUAL DICTATION

Talking about the weather can inspire dictation for individuals. Children can come by themselves and dictate to the teacher or an aide or even to a cassette tape recorder. They just might want to transcribe their feelings.

Having a "Poet's Bag" taped to the side of the desk is a good place to drop those tidbits that fall into one's consciousness. Later, if the children wish, time can be set aside for everyone to share these short poetic sayings. This is an excellent time to reward children with teacher praise.

GROUP DICTATION

Mood is an important aspect of poetic writing. When the sound of music plays softly from a record and the shades are drawn, the chances for poetic thinking and writing are heightened. There is a stimulation that passes from one to another, somewhat mystically. As one person grasps a perception, other minds intertwine with it. The perception grows into a concept and children begin to experience the fascination of logophiling.

A process of association feeds this experience. Here is a list of words that draw response. Try saying them in a darkened classroom:

moon

music

love

star

flower

apple

EXPERIENCING

The beginnings of poetic writing are rooted in the senses that children can explore within themselves. Touching, tasting, smelling, seeing, and hearing need to be reexplored and the experiences put into words.

See
Appendix
Item
1

Touching

walking barefoot in the sand and suddenly on hot pavement

feeling a small kitten

rolling down a grassy hill

diving into cold water

touching your way through a dark room

rubbing your fingers across sandpaper

squeezing a sponge full of water

sticking yourself with a needle while sewing

Tasting

pulling cotton candy and sticking it into your mouth

biting into a lemon

tasting cake frosting on a beater

peeling an orange with your teeth

drinking hot chocolate on a cold day

eating a dill pickle

crunching on dry cereal

holding a large ice cube in your mouth

Smelling

spraying perfume on your wrist

smelling the smoke of autumn leaves burning

walking into an attic closed for months

breathing deeply of a rose

passing by a disturbed skunk

taking down the Christmas tree as the pine needles fall

stepping into a bakery

Seeing

looking at the inside of a clock for the first time

watching the ferris wheel turn at the fair

observing dirt being taken from the carpet into the vacuum cleaner

staring at sparklers burning against a black sky

gazing at the sun setting slowly into the ocean

following the lines on the back of a maple leaf with your eyes

searching for a coin that rolled under the bed

squinting in the light after being in a dark room

Hearing

locating the cricket who wakes you from your sleep

feeling the door slam behind you when you meant to close it gently

listening to a lullaby on the radio that suddenly turns into a march

hearing the church bells toll twelve times

sensing the lonely wail of a river tugboat on a foggy night

lying in a bed while rain drops fall on the window panes

waiting for the sound of a car in the evening when a loved one is coming home from a long trip

recognizing the sound of the drill just before the dentist says, "Open wide, please"

> See
> Appendix
> Item
> 5

The more children hang around words the sooner they play with them. Perhaps the easiest way to encourage them is to have them print their names vertically and give the effect of association full reign. Using the five senses they can write poetic sense poems.

> See
> Appendix
> Item
> 21

JOHN SMITH: Touching

J   *John walked barefoot*

O   *over the*

H   *hot pavement.*

N   *Nothing is*

S   *so horrible he thought*

M   *miserably.*

I   *If I could only reach*

T   *the beach it wouldn't*

H   *hurt so much.*

Bring material to the classroom to touch, see, feel, taste, and hear. These concrete items generate vivid associations not garnered in any other way. Objects such as sticks, stones, dry seaweed, yarn, bottles, pencils, fruit, and clocks are useful in building word associations. List the objects and the words associated with them on a chalkboard or have the children write them in their notebooks. The word lists will be helpful in future poetic writing.

REMEMBERING

Our memories are often vivid and reflect experiences that were nurtured in emotion. They flit into our minds because of a chance remark, a smell, or a song. A feeling long forgotten may engulf us. These memories can form the basis of interesting poetic writing.

Sometimes the best way to bring these memories to the top of our minds is to seek the help of another person. Children can pair off to do this. One child is the writer/talker (w/t), the other, the questioner/listener (q/l). After pairing the children, write this question on the chalkboard: "What experience did you have when you were younger that was the happiest (or scariest, funniest) one you remember? Describe it."

As the w/t begins to share this experience with the q/l, the latter asks simple questions such as, How old were you then? Where did this happen? How did you feel? and so on. The q/l must not talk too much or the w/t will be distracted from writing. The w/t should soon start his or her writing as the q/l probes just enough to keep the writer progressing. When a short paragraph is written the two partners can change roles and begin again.

After their initial experiences are written down, each needs to take time to develop his or her material into poetic form.

Imagery

Imagery is the making of mental pictures. Images often flood our minds during sleep. Our daydreams give us mental pictures. Centuries ago people drew these mental pictures on the sides of caves. Now images are created electronically on glass tubes called television sets.

These images are pictures we see in our minds. The imagery of a poetic writing is stimulated by the written and verbal expressions of others. Comparisons are made.

> Shall I compare thee to a summer's day?
> Thou art more lovely and more temperate . . .
> *William Shakespeare (1564-1616)*

See
Appendix
Item
6

Written images are shortcuts to deeper meanings. Metaphors and similes are two types of imagery comparisons that enhance poetic writing.

Simile

The simile is a comparison of dissimilar things using *like* or *as*. The word comes from the Latin *similis* meaning similar. William Wordsworth (1770–1850) wrote that "Oft on the dappled turf at ease I sit, and play with similes." Here are two he played with:

Thy soul was like a star, and dwelt apart;
Thou hadst a voice whose sound was like the sea. . . .

Playing with similes is a good exercise for developing poetic writing with children. Here is a quasi-mathematical form to use.

_____ as _____

_____ like _____

Although the first tries may be clichés—"green as grass" or "I feel like a million"—encourage children to create crazy ones if they wish until the concept jells with them.

The cowbell is *like* my teacher.

A closed room is *like* my father's mind.

The sun beats down *as* an unrelenting tom-tom.

The wash on the line is *like* an egg being whipped into an omelet.

Metaphor

The ability to imply that a comparison exists is a metaphor. The term comes from the Greek, meaning "transference." For example, Romeo describes his Juliet by saying:

It is the east and Juliet is the sun.

Aristotle, in his *Poetics*, made much of the metaphor:

But by far the greatest thing is to be the master
of the metaphor. It is the one thing that cannot be
learned from others; and it is also an indication
of genius, since the ability to forge a good metaphor
shows that the poet has an intuitive perception of the
similarity in dissimilars.*

See
Appendix
Item
7

This form of imagery is somewhat more difficult to create than the simile. So you might start with the following format:

My head is a _____.

My dog is a _____.

The clouds are _____.

The candle is _____.

Then encourage the children to write metaphors similar to the examples that follow.

Aristotle's Poetics, translated by John Warrington (London: J.M. Dent & Sons Ltd., 1963), pp. 40–41.

My head is a *bomb*.

My dog is a *bowling ball*.

The clouds are *pillows*.

The candle is the *sun*.

FIGURATIVE COMPARISONS

The poet, Kenneth Koch, is a foremost exponent of comparison poems for children.* These forms are easily started and give children an early sense of poetic writing.

I used to _____ ,

But now _____ .

The "I used to/But now" format lets children turn back their thoughts to earlier times or just lets them invent fantastic thoughts.

I used to *like ice cream*,

But now *I eat only spinach*.

> See
> Appendix
> Item
> 8

The above leads into poetic writing without truth—the Lie Poem. Here the young writer is supposed to write an untruth in every line. This could also be called a Propaganda Poem—the way we would like things to be.

Reality must take leave at certain times so children can experience the joy of mental fantasy without guilt. How often all of us think "I am a _____ / But I wish I were _____." In this form anybody can wish to be somebody else. The comparisons are infinite.

> See
> Appendix
> Item
> 9

I am a *man*,
But I wish I were *a unicorn galloping through space*.

Another way to do the comparison poem is to use the words "If I were/I would." Here is an example:

If I were *a pony*,
I would *gallop down the Milky Way eating a Mars candy bar*.

> See
> Appendix
> Item
> 10

SOUND

There is more sound, noise if you please, surrounding us than we are capable of differentiating in a moment. Stop and listen for a minute,

*Kenneth Koch, *Wishes, Lies, and Dreams: Teaching Children to Write Poetry* (New York: Random House, 1970).

particularly if you are outside. Chances are you can list at least ten or more different sounds. Many of these sounds have their own peculiar rhythm and beat. Air conditioners, automobile engines, fans, bird calls, and fluorescent light bulbs insist on entering our subconscious and making a cumulative impression on us.

Rhythm

Rhythm is as natural as the heart beating seventy-two beats a minute, the tide ebbing and flowing off countless shorelines, the sun rising in the morning and setting in the evening. Rhythm is deeply ingrained in humans, particularly in young children. It comes out in body movements as they explore the space around them. It is found in the language they playfully use. Rhythm is a beat or accent that occurs with regularity in poetry.

Rhyme

When words find themselves at the end of lines with corresponding sounds (light-might; harpoon-baboon; reign-stain) the resonance of rhyming is taking place. This is one of the pleasant characteristics of poetry. Rhyming poetry, when done well, is wonderful to read. It should not be overemphasized when teaching children to express themselves poetically. But here are a couple of examples to read aloud. Many other rhyming words can be found in Appendix Item 39.

> A man of words and not of *deeds*
> Is like a garden full of *weeds*.

> Rain, rain, go *away*,
> Come again another *day*.

Meter

The pattern of a poem's rhythm is its meter. Formal poetry has a variety of measured beats. Some beats are quick and express joy and animation. Others are slower and give the feeling of mourning or deep reflection. The most common meters in English are (1) the iamb. *n.* (˘ ´) or iambic *adj.*—a metrical foot of two syllables, the first unaccented and the last accented.

How doth the little crocodile
Improve his shining tail,
And pour the waters of the Nile
On every golden scale!
How cheerfully he seems to grin,
How neatly spreads his claws,
And welcomes little fishes in
With gently smiling jaws!
Alice's Adventures in Wonderland
Lewis Carroll (1832-1898)

(2) the trochee *n.* (´ ˘) or trochaic *adj.*—a metrical foot of two syllables, the first accented and the last unaccented.

Bý thĕ shóres ŏf Gítchĕe Gúmĕe,
Bý thĕ shíniňg Bíg-Sĕa-Wátĕr,
Stóod thĕ wígwăm óf Ňokŏmĭs,
Dáughtĕr óf thĕ Moón, Ňokŏmĭs.
    "The Song of Hiawatha"
    Henry Wadsworth Longfellow (1807-1882)

(3) the anapest *n.* (˘ ˘ ´) or anapestic *adj.*—a metrical foot of three syllables, the first two unaccented and the last accented.

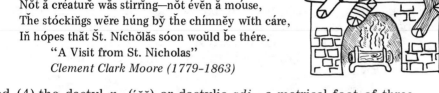

'Twăs thĕ níght bĕfŏre Chrístmăs,
Whĕn aíl thrŏugh thĕ hoúse
Nŏt ă créatŭrĕ wăs stírrĭng—nŏt évĕn ă moúse,
Thĕ stóckĭngs wĕre húng bў thĕ chímnĕy wĭth cáre,
Iň hópes thăt Št. Níchŏlăs sóon woŭld bĕ thére.
    "A Visit from St. Nicholas"
    Clement Clark Moore (1779-1863)

and (4) the dactyl *n.* (´ ˘ ˘) or dactylic *adj.*—a metrical foot of three syllables, the first accented and the last two unaccented.

Cánnŏn tŏ ríght ŏf thĕm,
Cánnŏn tŏ léft ŏf thĕm,
Cánnŏn iň frónt ŏf thĕm
    Vóllĕy'd aňd thúndeř'd.
Íntŏ thĕ jáws ŏf deăth,
Íntŏ thĕ moúth ŏf hĕll
    Róde thĕ sĭx húndrĕd.
    "The Charge of the Light Brigade"
    Alfred, Lord Tennyson (1809-1892)

Alliteration

Advertisements, both visual and auditory, bombard us with their alliterative sounds.

See
Appendix
Item
11

Big Big Sale!

Super Savings Special!

Terrific Times at Tysons!

This form of poetic writing, where consonants are repeated, is designed to make ruts in our memory banks so we will, for example, recall where the "Big Big Sale!" is taking place and go there to shop.

Children love to play verbally with the rhymes of Mother Goose, as in this couplet:

Pease-porridge hot, pease-porridge cold,
Pease-porridge in the pot, nine days old.

Alfred, Lord Tennyson used alliteration skillfully in *The Princess*. The alliteration is not confined to initial consonants but is also found in the medial and terminal positions.

Sweet is every sound,
Sweeter thy voice, but every sound is sweet;
Myriads of rivulets hurrying through the lawn,
The moan of doves in immemorial elms,
And murmuring of innumerable bees.

Help children to recognize alliteration by finding it in newspapers and magazines and listening for it on radio and television. As they become tuned into this facet of poetic writing and sound, encourage them to include it in their own poetic expressions.

Free Verse

See
Appendix
Item
12

As the chorus in a classical Greek drama circled the stage chanting an ode, the audience felt the cadence, balance, and rhythm. The movement of the chorus became known as the *strophe* from which we get *strophic rhythm*. Strophic rhythm differs from the formal rhythm of poetry because of its irregularity. The emotional and thoughtful stresses dictated by the content of poetic writing determine the balance, cadence, and rhythm by which the material will be read; hence, the concept of free verse.

Hebrew Biblical writers wrote in this cadenced verse. The great literature of the Psalms, Song of Solomon, and Job are excellent examples. The format of the writing often determines the rhythm and, consequently, how well the material will be understood. For instance, a selection from the Book of Job, Chapter 38, verses 4 through 7, looks this way when found in the traditional format.

> 4 Where wast thou when I laid the founda-
> tions of the earth? declare, if thou hast under-
> standing.
>   5. Who hath laid the measures thereof, if thou
> knowest? or who hath stretched the line upon
> it?
>   6 Whereupon are the foundations thereof
> fastened? or who laid the corner stone thereof;
>   7 When the morning stars sang together, and
> all the sons of God shouted for joy?

But when the same words are arranged by line as follows, the rhythm and cadence of the material seems to be freed of its printed constraints. Meaning has more of a chance to flow from the page.

> Where wast thou
> When I laid the foundations of the earth?
> Declare,
> If thou hast understanding.
> Who hath laid the measurement thereof,
> If thou knowest?
> Or who hath stretched the line upon it?
> Whereupon are the foundations thereof fastened?
> Or who laid the cornerstone thereof
> When the morning stars sang together
> And all the sons of God shouted for joy?

Walt Whitman (1819–1892) was called "the father of the free verse movement" by some. Other well-known writers of free verse were Amy Lowell, Matthew Arnold, and Carl Sandburg. Walt Whitman had an unusual ability to make the simplest concepts profound in free verse.

I believe a leaf of grass is no less than the journey-work
    of the stars,
And the pismire* is equally perfect, and a grain of sand
    and the egg of the wren,
And the tree-toad is a chef-d'oeuvre† of the highest,
And the running blackberry would adorn the parlors of
    heaven,
And the narrowest hinge in my hand puts to scorn all
    machinery,
And the cow, crunching with depress'd head, surpasses
    any statue,
And a mouse is miracle enough to stagger sextillions
    of infidels. . . .

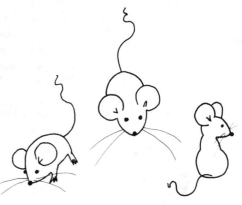

Whitman draws us into the world of common things and lets us see their uncommoness. Children need the daily practice of viewing the world around them. This can be accomplished by taking a few moments each day to tell in a few words what was seen recently, even that morning, that was beautiful or unusual. You might start off by saying you saw the dew sparkle on a leaf of grass, an oil slick in the driveway, an inch worm, a candle flicker, or a salamander scurry across the porch. As these experiences are described in more detail, the children will soon pick up on them. This microscopic look at the common can then be translated into free verse and other poetic forms. But it must be done consistently to become an habitual part of the children's poetic view of the world.

POETIC SHAPES

Poetic writing sends signals through its content on how it should be shaped by line breaks and spacing. While sound is generally considered most important, entertaining the eyes falls a close second.

Prose/Poetry

Children can practice poetic shaping by choosing prose they enjoy or prose they write and, then, through arranging and rearranging the lines, phrases, and words, give the prose the look of poetry. Biblical writing and fine literature of the past and present, written in prose, make good practice for poetic writing. The Preamble to the Constitution of the United States is an excellent place to start.

*an ant
†masterpiece

We, the people of the United States,
in order to form
a more perfect Union,
establish justice,
insure domestic tranquility,
provide for the common defense,
and
secure the blessings of liberty
to ourselves
and our posterity,
do ordain and establish
this Constitution
for the
United States of America.

Here is a list of other writings* to practice shaping into poetic form by line and spacing.

Address at Gettysburg, November 19, 1863 by Abraham Lincoln

The Adventures of Tom Sawyer, Chapter 2 (whitewashing the fence) by Mark Twain

Speech on Dunkirk, June 4, 1940, House of Commons by Sir Winston Churchill

The Sea Around Us by Rachel Carson

See
Appendix
Item
13, 14, 15

CONCRETE POETRY

The step between poetic writing and poetic drawing is concrete poetry or, as it is often called, picture poetry. The writers use the letters, words, and sentences to form the poetic images and ideas they want to convey.

*See the latest edition (1980) of John Bartlett, *Familiar Quotations* (Boston: Little, Brown) for these and other excellent writings to shape into poetic form.

```
   like      attracts     like *
   like      attracts     like
   like      attracts     like
    like     attracts    like
    like    attracts    like
     like   attracts   like
      like attracts like
       likeattractslike
        likeattractlike
         likattraclike
          liketraclike
           likeralike
            likelikts
```

All children can be involved in this type of poetic writing since it is primarily a visual form of poetry, although some concrete poems are read.

Forms of concrete poetry can be traced back to the anagrams of early Christian monks and poets. Lewis Carroll produced picture poetry in his "Mouse's Tale" from *Alice in Wonderland*.

```
"Fury said to
 a mouse, That
  he met in the
    house, 'Let
      us both go
       to law: I
        will prose-
         cute you.—
          Come, I'll
          take no de-
         nial: We
        must have
       the trial;
      For really
    this morn-
    ing I've
    nothing
    to do.'
    Said the
     mouse to
      the cur,
       Such a
        trial, dear
         sir, With
          no jury
           or judge,
            would
            be wast-
           ing our
          breath.
         I'll be
        judge,
       I'll be
       jury,'
       said
      cun-
      ning
      old
      Fury:
       'I'll
        try
         the
          whole
           cause,
            and
            con-
           demn
          you to
         death.
```

Concrete poetry takes various shapes and is only hampered by one's lack of imagination and creativity.

```
    .enderness s-
    .elf-consciousness
     isolation temper bigo
     igotry disgust greed ha
     .ate restlessness lust stup
    elfishness frustration igner
    sanity gregariousness lonelin
    difference pride doubt fear en
    aivete injustice curiosity conf
    mper indifference LOVE jealous
    nderness self-consciousness fe
    olation temper bigotry disgust
    reed hate restlessness lust ha
    upidity selfishness frustratio
    norance insanity loneliness pr
     difference doubt fear envy i
     justice naivete curiosity
     tenderness self-consicou
     solation frustration
     reed hate restlessn
     solation temper big
     aivete inju-*i-- -
     curiosity
     nvy temper
     ride do
       ide
```

*Emmett Williams, *An Anthology of Concrete Poetry* (New York: Something Else Press, Inc. 1967), unpaged. Reprinted by permission.

NUMBER POEMS

Children prefer structure to freedom without guidance. This not only holds true with discipline but also with writing. Number poems give them constraints to work within, but also allow creativity to flow.

There are numerous types of number poem structures to follow. After doing several, children will soon make up their own. This type of poetic writing can be written in syllables or in words.

License Plate Poems

<table>
<tr><td>See
Appendix
Item
16</td></tr>
</table>

Before beginning to write this type of poem, have the children bring in the license plate numbers from their parents' cars or those they see on the street. For example, if the license plate is M 417 D, have them write the number vertically on a sheet of paper. After the letters, they write words beginning with those letters. After the numbers, they write words that total the number of syllables or the number of words indicated by the numbers. The following illustrations are by syllables.

M 417 D

M   My

4   age is against

1   me.

7   Being nine is too young to

D   drive.

SIG 674

S   Summer

I   is

G   gone.

6   The trees react trembling,

7   sending showers of color.

4   Winter beckons.

Address Poems

<table>
<tr><td>See
Appendix
Item
17</td></tr>
</table>

Making an address poem can fix an address in a youngster's mind, if he or she tends to forget it. Since addresses are longer than license plate numbers, divide the address into parts and have the class decide on using words or syllables or both. For instance, if the address contains abbreviations such as S. (South) W. (West) or St. (Street), just use the initials and not the whole word as in the following example:

4443 S.E. 47 Dr.

4   Waffles are my

4   favorite food.

4   I eat them with

3   butter and

S.   syrup,

E.   even

4   good brown gravy.

7   They also taste scrumptious with

D   delicious

r.   raspberries.

The names of cities and states are additions to consider with address poems. Some children find challenge in their poetic writing by using their grandparents' addresses or those of favorite aunts and uncles. They can then have the additional experience of addressing envelopes and sending their poetry to their relatives.

Other sources for this form of poetic writing are locker numbers, telephone numbers, social security numbers, bicycle registration numbers, or any numbers that are part of everyday life.

> See
> Appendix
> Item
> 18

NOUN AND VERB POEMS

Noun and verb poems are arranged to portray the meanings of the words themselves. To form these poems, just arrange the letters of the word or words in the form of the word's meaning.

Action verbs are particularly good to start off with.

> See
> Appendix
> Item
> 19

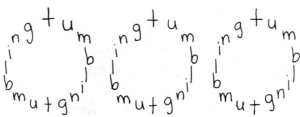

Here are some others to try.

flying	falling
snooping	stepping
looking	crying
sneezing	smiling

See
Appendix
Item
20

Once the children get the idea of verb poems, have them try noun poems.

airplane	*airplane*	school
dog		automobile
cat		football
chair		tree

Word groups are the next step. By making *prancing* an adjective, the word group becomes *prancing horses*. *Tumbling* as an adjective becomes *tumbling tumbleweed*.

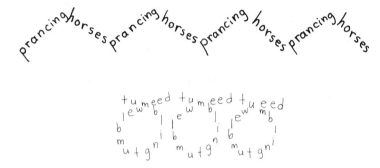

NAME POEMS

See
Appendix
Item
21

Name poems are descriptive of how a person would like to think he or she is perceived by others. These poems are written as one-word descriptions or in sentence form. First, middle, or last names can comprise a poem. A dictionary helps as does skimming through newspapers and magazines.

R	reasonable
U	useful
T	terrific
H	helpful
D	dedicated
E	energetic
N	neighborly
I	intelligent
S	special
E	entertaining
J	joyful
E	eager
A	able
N	neat
N	necessary
E	ethical

Children can make poems more specific by finding words that describe how they think they are thought of by their teacher, principal, mother, father, brother, sister, or best friend.

NEWSPAPER POEMS

Finding poetic writing in newspapers is comparatively simple. Have children cut out a number of words and word groups that appeal to them from headlines and advertisements. Then have the children arrange these on their desks until they create a poem that states a message they want to express. The words are then pasted on a separate sheet of paper.

See Appendix Item 22

Another way is to have children cut a variety of paragraphs from articles in the newspaper. With a pencil or marking pen, they underline words or word groups that appeal to them, rewriting the words in poetic form.

TWO-WORD POEMS

See Appendix Item 23

The simplicity of two-word poems helps children to not only be descriptive in their poetic writing but also develop quantity. The only rule to follow is that each line has only two words. The poems can be as long or as short as desired.

My father

Strong arms

Thin face

Definite opinions

Hard worker

Family man

See Appendix Item 24

My mother

Very soft

Beautiful eyes

Strong willed

Financial genius

Loves children

CHAPTER 3

If I were a Queen,
    What would I do?
I'd make you King,
    And I'd wait on you.

If I were a King,
    What would I do?
I'd make you Queen,
    For I'd marry you.

Christina Georgina Rossetti (1830–1894)

DEVELOPING LANGUAGE PRECISION

Poetic writing demands preciseness. The word *precise* embodies the ideas of delineation and limit. Writing poetically helps children develop this language skill.

HAIKU

The masters of preciseness are the Japanese. This ability is epitomized in their gardens, homes, methods of food preparation, industry, and in poetic language. The one language form where this is especially true is the *haiku*, which has been esteemed by the Japanese for many centuries.

The classical haiku, first called *hokku* or starting verse, deals with a season of the year. In the poem the poet hints about the season through a word or context, either directly or indirectly. Two other requirements, which are not always rigidly adhered to, are the concern with a specific event and presenting that event as being in the act of happening.

One good point about the haiku is that the form is simple, disciplined, and nonrhyming. Haiku serves as an excellent way to introduce children to writing poetry.

The simplicity of the form centers in its syllable count. Haiku has seventeen syllables divided in lines of five, seven, and five syllables.

> See
> Appendix
> Item
> 25

———————— 5

—————————— 7

———————— 5

The seventeen syllable count serves as a guide for writing a haiku; it is not a stringent, inflexible rule. Young children will need more leeway than older children.

The best of haiku lets the reader draw conclusions through subtlety, not bald statements of fact.* The following haikus were written by children many years ago and just recently translated by Dr. Takashi Hasegawa, Professor of Japanese Language and Literature, Hyogo University of Teacher Education.†

Gentle waterfall,
Tripping over rocks and stones
Creating beauty.

Dew forms in gardens!
Emerald plants burst gaily,
As sunlight breaks through.

Scarlet cardinal
Standing in the soft white snow;
Flies away swiftly.

Rain clouds hang heavy!
Lightning strikes while thunder roars!
Rain patters softly. . . .

TANKA

Haiku originally was only the start of a poem called the *tanka*. The tanka gives a more complete view of the poet's thoughts by adding two more lines of seven syllables.

> See
> Appendix
> Item
> 26

_____5

_____7   hokku

_____5

_____7

_____7   ageku

The first three lines are the haiku or hokku (starting verse). The last two lines are the *ageku* which give a finality or conclusive quality to the tanka.

*See Bibliographies for books on haiku, especially those of Harold G. Henderson.

†The author is indebted to Dr. Tatsumi Ueno of Hyogo University of Teacher Education, Japan for making the translations possible.

RENGA

The *renga* is a form linking the haiku and tanka where a number of poets alternate in writing. In a classroom one child could write the haiku starting verse (5,7,5); the next child, the completed tanka (7,7); the next a haiku following the theme set forth (5,7,5); and so on.

See
Appendix
Item
27

> When I'm on the farm
> My mornings are filled with work.
> The cows need feeding
>
> The chickens scratch for their food
> And pigs grunt through sleepy eyes.
>
> But in my own home
> My mornings are different.
> The dog needs to walk.
>
> My cat purrs for her food dish
> And I grunt through sleepy eyes.

SENRYU

A Japanese poet originated the *senryu* that carries his name. The syllabic form of the haiku is present in the senryu. The major difference is that the senryu is not confined to a season of the year or to nature. In this form children can write on any subject they wish, that is, specific sports, foods, people, or hobbies. Often what passes for haiku in the classroom is actually a senryu.

See
Appendix
Item
28

> The little white ball
> Pops gingerly along . . . waits
> For me at first—OUT!

LANTERNE

The lanterne contains five lines in the general shape of a Japanese lantern. The form is a simple poetic device lending itself to artistic illustration.

See
Appendix
Item
29

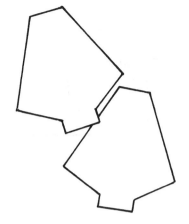

Line	Syllables	Shape
1.	1	—
2.	2	— —
3.	3	— — —
4.	4	— — — —
5.	1	—

My
puppy
black and white
soft, cuddly, fur
mine.

CHAIN LANTERNE

See
Appendix
Item
30

A chain lanterne is a simple lanterne repeated following the original theme. These can go on and on and offer not only interesting poetic writing experiences for children but also creative art projects upon which to display students' writing.

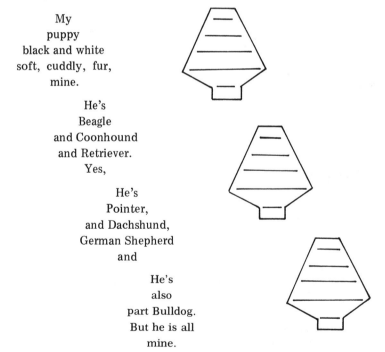

My
puppy
black and white
soft, cuddly, fur,
mine.

He's
Beagle
and Coonhound
and Retriever.
Yes,

He's
Pointer,
and Dachshund,
German Shepherd
and

He's
also
part Bulldog.
But he is all
mine.

CINQUAIN

The *cinquain* (SIN-kane) is a five-line poem. The French word, *cinq* for five, is the basis for the name. The creator was Adelaide Crapsey, a young American woman fluent in French. She was influenced a great deal by the Japanese haiku and tanka and decided to make an

American poem to parallel the haiku. Miss Crapsey was ill much of her young adult life and died in 1914 at the age of 36. She invented the cinquain in 1911, although she never lived to see those she wrote in print.

Miss Crapsey may not have considered the cinquain a syllabic form of poetry, nevertheless, it has become that, particularly with children. Her cinquains are metaphors, building in intensity and then falling away.

*The Warning**

Just now,
Out of the strange
Still dusk . . . as strange, as still . . .
A white moth flew, Why am I grown
So cold?

Adelaide Crapsey (1878-1914)

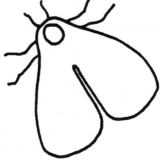

See
Appendix
Item
31

The cinquain as used with children follows the pattern below:

_____ 2 syllables   title

_____ 4 syllables   description of title

_____ 6 syllables   action

_____ 8 syllables   feeling

_____ 2 syllables   another word for the title

Flowers
Yellow, dark red
Waving in the morning
Their fragrance brings me happiness
Roses

CHAIN CINQUAIN

A chain cinquain is a series of cinquains following each other based on a single theme. Children can write letters or notes to friends and relatives in this format.

See
Appendix
Item
32

*Adelaide Crapsey, *Verse* (Rochester, N.Y.: The Manas Press, 1915), p. 46.

See
Appendix
Item
33

DOUBLE CINQUAIN

By doubling syllables in each line a double cinquain is formed. This form begins to approximate prose and can be a method for moving into the study and practice of paragraph writing.

_____ 4

_____ 8

_____ 12

_____ 16

_____ 4

Oak tree, gnarled trunk
Clutching earth, reaching for the sun.
You have been here since Indians have passed your feet
Watching men divide earth and grasp for footholds in highest heaven.
What thoughts you have.

DIAMANTE

The _diamante_ (dee-ah-MAHN-tay) was created by Iris M. Tiedt.* The first and last words are opposites such as boys and girls, or rocks and sand. There are seven lines in the diamante, each with its own requirements.

See
Appendix
Item
34

Line	_Requirements_
1.	one-word subject: noun, opposite of word in last line
2.	two words: adjectives describing subject in first line
3.	three words: participles: _-ing, -ed_ words about subject in first line
4.	four words: nouns about subject in first and last lines
5.	three words: participles; _-ing, -ed_ words about subject in last line
6.	two words: adjectives describing subject in last line
7.	one-word subject: noun, opposite of word in first line

rocks
hard, flinty
falling, cascading, hurting
mountains, buildings, beaches, concrete
shifting, slippery, changing
gritty, coarse
sand

*Iris M. Tiedt, "A New Poetry Form: The Diamante," _Elementary English_ 46 (May, 1969), pp. 588-589.

Here are a few antonyms to get your class started. Later, duplicate Appendix 34 or write selected antonyms on the chalkboard for the children.

See
Appendix
Item
35

admit	deny	finish	begin
argue	agree	hate	love
break	mend	knowledge	ignorance
busy	idle	lift	drop
catch	release	lively	slow
choose	refuse	quiet	excited
clean	dirty	right	wrong
coax	repel	strong	weak
collect	scatter	sticky	dry
compel	hinder	true	false

PROVERBS

Down through the centuries proverbs have found their way as a means of expressing some truth or observation in a short, somewhat pithy manner. These sayings have become so popular and familiar that they take on a cliché-like quality.

Rain before seven,
Fair by eleven.

Often proverbs are spoken as similes.

She is "as sharp as a needle."
He is "as bright as a new pin."

Some proverbs express well-known truths.

Tommy's tears, and Mary's fears,
Will make them old before their years.

Proverbs are among the oldest poetic works dating back to Sanskrit, Hebrew, Germanic, and Scandanavian literature. Geoffrey Chaucer, the fourteenth century English poet of *The Canterbury Tales*, commonly used them. The appeal of proverbs is universal because of the literary forms they embody.

Metaphor
Still waters run deep

Parallel structure
Man proposes,
God disposes.

The prodigal robs his heir,
the miser robs himself.

Rhyme

A friend in need
is a friend indeed.

A sunshiny shower
Won't last half an hour.

Play on words

Forewarned, forearmed.

Proverbs cover a wide range of interests including home remedies for illnesses, practical living, weather, and superstition.

Home Remedies

Feed a cold, starve a fever.

Practical Living

Time and tide wait for no man.

A man of words, and not of deeds,
Is like a garden full of weeds;
For when the weeds begin to grow,
Then doth the garden overflow.

He that would thrive
Must rise at five;
He that hath thriven
May lie till seven;
And he that by the plough would thrive,
Himself must either hold or drive.

For want of a nail, the shoe was lost;
For want of the shoe, the horse was lost;
For want of the horse, the rider was lost;
For want of the rider, the battle was lost;
For want of the battle, the kingdom was lost;
And all from the want of a horseshoe nail.

Kind hearts are the gardens,
    Kind thoughts are the roots,
Kind words are the blossoms,
    Kind deeds are the fruits;
Love is the sweet sunshine
    That warms into life,
For only in darkness
    Grow hatred and strife.

They that wash on Monday
Have all the week to dry;
They that wash on Tuesday
Are not so much awry;
They that wash on Wednesday
Are not so much to blame;
They that wash on Thursday,
Wash for shame;
They that wash on Friday,
Wash in need;
And they that wash on Saturday,
Oh, they are slovens, indeed.

Weather

March winds and April showers
Bring forth May flowers.

Rainbow at night
Is the sailor's delight;
Rainbow at morning,
Sailors, take warning.

Evening red and morning gray
Set the traveller on his way,
But evening gray and morning red,
Bring the rain upon his head.

The South wind brings wet weather,
The North wind wet and cold together;
The West wind always brings us rain,
The East wind blows it back again.

Superstitions

See a pin and pick it up,
All the day you'll have good luck;
See a pin and let it lay,
Bad luck you will have all day.

Marry Monday, marry for wealth;
Marry Tuesday, marry for health;
Marry Wednesday, the best day of all;
Marry Thursday, marry for crosses;
Marry Friday, marry for losses;
Marry Saturday, no luck at all.

Sneeze on a Monday, you sneeze for danger;
Sneeze on a Tuesday, you'll kiss a stranger;
Sneeze on a Wednesday, you sneeze for a letter;
Sneeze on a Thursday, for something better;
Sneeze on a Friday, you sneeze for sorrow;
Sneeze on a Saturday, your sweetheart tomorrow;
Sneeze on a Sunday, your safety seek—
The devil will have you the whole of the week.

As children learn proverbs and take them home to parents and grandparents, many others will come back to class. As these are written and duplicated for classroom use, it is then a small step towards children writing their own. Practical living themes abound in the Boy Scout Laws:

Trustworthy	Obedient
Loyal	Cheerful
Helpful	Thrifty
Friendly	Brave
Courteous	Clean
Kind	Reverent

Other values serving as the basis of themes for proverbs are: love, beauty, brotherhood, courage, patience, democracy, dependability, freedom, peace, promptness, responsibility, liberty, and industry.

PARALLELISM

As proverbs were passed from one culture to another, through many generations and various languages, some were so universal in their application to the condition of men and women that it was evident that the qualities they possessed would not let them pass through the cracks of time and be forgotten. They took on the classification of "learned proverbs." This genre of proverbs was made famous by King Solomon of Old Testament fame who wrote the Book of Proverbs. Many of these proverbs are written in parallel structure, that is, the first line compares or contrasts with the second.

Synonymous Parallelism

Parallelism as a technique is not only used in lines of two or couplets, but even in paragraph forms. However, it is probably better to introduce parallelism to children with two-line poems. In synonymous parallelism the first line states a fact. The second line does the same with different words that contribute the same meaning or thought as the first line. Here are some examples from the Book of Solomon in the Bible:

> Let thine eyes look right on,
> and let thine eyelids look straight before thee.
> > Proverbs 4:25

> Give instruction to a wise man, and he will be yet wiser:
> teach a just man, and he will increase in learning.
> > Proverbs 9:10

> My son, keep thy father's commandments,
> and forsake not the law of thy mother.
> > Proverbs 6:20

See
Appendix
Item
36

After reading several proverbs let the children write some in the same style. For example, following the theme of obedience—

Children obey your fathers
and obey your mothers, also.

From here they can go on to their own proverbs and, perhaps, write something like the following in the style of synonymous parallelism.

Books are gates opening to a larger world;
The print unlocks the pages to open lands.

As children learn to write in two-line synonymous parallelisms, encourage them to write sequentially with a theme. In this way they can develop their poetic ability in a quantitative sense.

Walt Whitman, the master of free verse, used this technique with great sensitivity.

I think I could turn and live with animals, they are so
     placid and self-contain'd,
I stand and look at them and long and long.
They do not sweat and whine about their condition,
They do not lie awake in the dark and weep for their sins,
They do not make me sick discussing their duty to God,
Not one is dissatisfied, not one is demented with the mania
     of owning things,
Not one kneels to another, nor to his kind that lived
     thousands of years ago,
Not one is respectable or unhappy over the whole earth.

Antithetic Parallelism

Antithetic means the direct opposite or contrast. In antithetic parallelism as a poetic technique, the first sentence states a fact but the second line, instead of contributing to the meaning with a similar thought, actually gives an opposite or dissimilar view. Solomon also used this technique:

See
Appendix
Item
37

A wise son maketh a glad father:
But a foolish son is the heaviness of his mother.
    Proverbs 10:1

Every wise woman buildeth her house;
but the foolish plucketh it down with her hands.
    Proverbs 14:1

A tablebearer revealeth secrets;
but he that is of a faithful spirit concealeth the matter.
    Proverbs 11:13

A soft answer turneth away wrath:
but grievous words stir up anger.
    Proverbs 15:1

The list of antonyms in Appendix Item 35 should give children a great number of ideas for developing their proverbs using antithetic parallelism. Here are two examples suggested from that list:

A *friend* stands ready to help
While a *foe* turns his back.

It is better to think *big* and gain a little
Than to think *little* and gain nothing at all.

APPROXIMATION POEMS

See Appendix Item 38

Reading poetry until it becomes part of oneself is the only way to develop some depth of understanding of poetic style. To write poetry children ought to have opportunities to approximate the styles of various poets until that special "feel" for poetry takes hold. The styles of the children will emerge in great varieties just as they do in handwriting, even though all the letters are standardized.

As a technique, writers sometimes approximate styles to get the feel for a particular market in which they want to be published. For instance, a writer will read a number of issues of a specific magazine to determine the types of articles and the general style editors select for the magazine. Some writers actually copy several pages from the periodical in longhand to get more familiar with what the editor wants.

To get "set" poetically, children can (1) read the works of certain poets and then approximate their styles; (2) write the poet's poetry by hand; (3) change the rhyme scheme or specific words, if they wish; and (4) approximate their own poems to the same rhythm of the poet. This writing will parallel the poet's writing on the page.

A simple example to begin with and one children already parody is "Roses Are Red."

Roses are red,   Roses are red,
Violets are blue,   Violets are blue,
Sugar is sweet   Brother made soup
And so are you.   With my old shoe.

RHYMES

See Appendix Item 39

Children love to hear and say rhyming poems. However, a forced rhyme may turn exciting poetic writing into doggerel. One way of reducing this possibility is to give children many rhyme options. Duplicate the list of rhyming words in Appendix Item 39 for the children's use and write rhyming words on the chalkboard when introducing rhyming poetry. Rhyming dictionaries are also excellent sources of rhyming words.

There are three common schemes that are most suitable to use with children: couplets, triplets, and quatrains.

Couplet

A couplet is a pair of rhymes. The lines match in length, rhyme, or both. Couplets have a long history. Some were used to teach children to read in the 1700s. *The New England Primer* contained these couplets:

In Adam's fall
We sinned all.

My Book and Heart
Must never part.

Xerxes did die,
And so must I.

Here is a favorite couplet generally sung on Saturdays:

Rain, rain, go away,
Come again another day.

And children jump and skip to this one:

Jumping Jack, jumping Jack,
Missed a crack and broke his back.

Start children on couplets by first reading them aloud and then putting rhyming words on the chalkboard as below:

_____ find

_____ mind

_____ shaken

_____ taken

_____ knock

_____ rock

_____ simmer

_____ trimmer

See
Appendix
Item
40

Triplet

The triplet, or tercet as it is sometimes called, is a stanza of three lines. The lines may rhyme or not. Tennyson used the triplet pattern in "The Eagle."

> He clasps the crag with crooked hands;
> Close to the sun in lonely lands,
> Ring'd with the azure world he stands.
>
> The wrinkled sea beneath him crawls;
> He watches from his mountain walls,
> And like a thunderbolt he falls.

The couplet "Rain, rain, go away," is often recited as a triplet with an additional line:

> Rain, rain, go away,
> Come again another day,
> Little Tommie wants to play.

There are a number of triplets coming out of the Mother Goose tradition:

> Jack be nimble,
> Jack be quick,
> Jack, jump over the candlestick.

> Jingle bells, jingle bells, jingle all the way,
> Oh what fun it is to ride
> In a one-horse open sleigh!

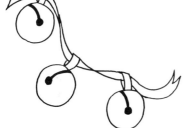

> Shoe a little horse,
> Shoe a little mare,
> But let the little colt go bare, bare, bare.

Rhyming patterns of triplets vary. The examples below indicate by letter how the lines of a triplet can be rhyming or nonrhyming.

See
Appendix
Item
41

1 _____ a	1 _____ a
2 _____ a	2 _____ a
3 _____ a	3 _____ b

1 _____ a	1 _____ a
2 _____ b	2 _____ b
3 _____ a	3 _____ b

Some authorities consider the haiku a triplet. Therefore, and for the purpose of encouraging children to write poetically, none of the lines of a triplet need rhyme to be acceptable in this category.

Quatrain

The quatrain is the most common form of poetry. Its four lines may have any rhythm although the iambic (Jĕllô) and trochaic (brôthĕr) are the least difficult for youngsters interested and able to put their writing in meter. The last line is rhymed with the second or third to give unity to the quatrain. The rhyme schemes of the quatrain are:

1 _____ a	1 _____ a
2 _____ a	2 _____ b
3 _____ b	3 _____ a
4 _____ b	4 _____ b

1 _____ a	1 _____ a
2 _____ b	2 _____ b
3 _____ c	3 _____ b
4 _____ b	4 _____ a

See
Appendix
Item
42

You may wish to introduce this form by reading a couplet and then letting the children compose the next two lines.

Here are two poems by Emily Dickinson (1830–1886) in the quatrain format.

Pedigree

The pedigree of honey
    Does not concern the bee;
A clover, anytime, to him
    Is aristocracy.

Chartless

I never saw a moor,
I never saw the sea;
Yet know I how the heather looks,
And what a wave must be.

I never spoke with God,
Nor visited in Heaven;
Yet certain am I of the spot
As if the chart were given.

EPITAPHS, EPIGRAMS, AND JINGLES

There are three forms that use the basic rhyme and rhythm patterns of couplets, triplets, and quatrains. Often it is difficult to separate them from one another unless you see the one on a tombstone; then you know it is an epitaph. All three can be pleasurable writing experiences for children.

Epitaph

See
Appendix
Item
43

An epitaph is an inscription on a tombstone or monument in memory of the one buried there. It commemorates or epitomizes the deceased. The earliest epitaphs are found on Egyptian coffins. But even today a walk through an old cemetery will turn up poignant epitaphs as this one:

It is so soon that I am done for,
I wonder what I was begun for.

And then there are the amusing ones that could serve as catylysts and motivation for further writing by children:

This is the grave of Mike O'Day
Who died maintaining his right of way.
His right was clear, his will was strong
But he's just as dead as if he'd been wrong.

Epigram

An epigram is a brief, pointed, and witty single thought. It is often antithetical as in "Man proposes but God disposes." The epigram is generally a couplet or quatrain. There is a more personal quality to epigrams than proverbs and often an element of surprise is found in the last line.

Matthew Prior, an English poet and diplomat (1664–1721) is remembered for his humorous light verse. Here is one of his epigrams:

> Sir, I admit your general rule,
> That every poet is a fool:
> But you yourself may serve to show it,
> That every fool is not a poet.

Jingles

Jingles are short, catchy poems with repetitions of sounds in rhyme or alliteration. Often, they do not even make sense. They lend themselves to repetition and are memorized easily. Here are two that are particularly well known:

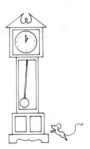

> Hickory dickory dock,
> The mouse ran up the clock
> The clock struck one,
> The mouse ran down
> Hickory dickory dock.

> Eeny, meeny, miny, mo
> Catch a tiger by his toe;
> If he squeals, let him go,
> Eeny, meeny, miny, mo.

LIMERICK

On May 12, 1812, Mrs. Lear gave birth to her last child, number 21. His name was Edward. Little did she realize her son would be recognized as the popularizer of the limerick, a five-line, humorous poem. Perhaps being around so many brothers and sisters during his life gave Edward Lear many things to write about. As a result, his verses were published in 1864 under the title, *A Book of Nonsense.*

Edward Lear was also an excellent artist. He drew birds, animals, plants, and medical sketches. With these two gifts, art and the limerick, he entertained many children.

Lear's limericks depend on a sort of wildness and craziness of thought to put across their humor.

There was an old man with a beard,
Who said, "It is just as I feared,
Two owls and a hen,
Four larks and a wren,
Have all built their nests in my beard."

A limerick from a later unknown writer gives a humorous twist in the fifth line.

There was an old man of Nantucket,
Who kept all his cash in a bucket;
But his daughter, named Nan,
Ran away with a man,
And as for the bucket—Nantucket.

Oliver Wendell Holmes (1809–1894) did the same thing with his limerick "Eggstravagance." Note carefully the endings of the first and last lines.

The Reverend Henry Ward Beecher
Called a hen a most elegant creature,
The hen, pleased with that,
Laid an egg in his hat—
And thus did the hen reward Beecher!

The rhyme scheme of lines 1, 2, and 5 rhyming, and 3 and 4 rhyming is illustrated below.

1 _____ a

2 _____ a

3 _____ b

4 _____ b

5 _____ a

While limericks are noted for their humor, you should be careful when reading them aloud. Some are written in a bawdy, earthy style. As with all material read to children, preread limericks for content and appropriateness.

Here are some limericks to read aloud until appropriate books are found in libraries and bookstores.

There was an old man from Peru
Who dreamed he was eating his shoe;
    He woke in a fright
    In the middle of the night
And found it was perfectly true.

    Anonymous

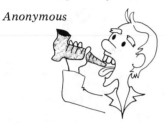

There was an old man of Blackheath,
Who sat on his set of false teeth.
    Said he, with a start,
    "Oh, Lord, bless my heart!
I've bitten myself underneath!"

    Anonymous

I raised a great hullabaloo
When I found a large mouse in my stew,
    Said the waiter, "Don't shout
    And wave it about,
Or the rest will be wanting one too!"

    Anonymous

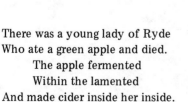

There was a young lady of Ryde
Who ate a green apple and died.
    The apple fermented
    Within the lamented
And made cider inside her inside.

    Anonymous

There was a young lady of Niger
Who smiled as she rode on a tiger;
> They returned from the ride
> With the lady inside,
And the smile on the face of the tiger.

> *Anonymous*

There was an old man in a tree,
Whose whiskers were lovely to see.
> But the birds of the air
> Plucked them perfectly bare,
To make themselves nests in that tree.

> *Edward Lear*

There is a young lady, whose nose,
Continually prospers and grows.
> When it grew out of sight,
> She exclaimed in a fright,
"Oh, Farewell to the end of my nose!"

> *Edward Lear*

Children have little difficulty making up their own limericks after hearing a few of them read aloud. Before finishing reading a fifth line, let the class try to guess the rhyming word or actually give their own last sentence. You can also give them a first line and then list words together on the chalkboard that rhyme with the word. Appendix Item 39 is helpful when doing this activity.* For starters, try these first lines:

There once was a boy with a bell

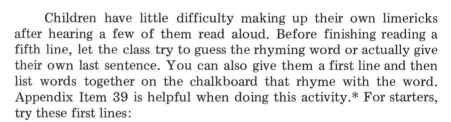

*For information on setting up a limerick center in the classroom see Mary McDonald Harris, "The Limerick Center," *Language Arts* 53 (September, 1976), pp. 663–665.

There was a young girl with an ache

There once was a man who was bald

Across a wide lake a man swam

The cost of a young centipede

The two of them went on a cruise

She fancied herself a good swimmer

CHAPTER 4

I have just heard a poem spoken
with so delicate a sense of its
rhythm, with so perfect a respect
for its meaning, that if
I were a wise man and could persuade
a few people to learn the art
I would never open a book of
verse again.

William Butler Yeats (1865–1939)

SHARING POETIC WRITING

Poetry is meant to be read aloud. Its rhythm, cadence, meter, rhyme, and alliteration, are locked tightly in type until someone frees it for all to enjoy.

Poetry is meant to be heard. Children should hear poetry every day. There is not a subject area that cannot be introduced with an appropriate poem. Anthologies abound with poetic classifications from which to choose.

Children's poetic writing is meant to be read aloud, if they so desire. The act of sharing is an incentive to write more. Continuing interaction with poetry helps children view the world with empathy, concern, and, perhaps, gain some creative insights on how to solve or live more comfortably with its problems.

ORAL SHARING

The reading of poetry and poetic writing is a center-stage activity; not "off the cuff" but a specific, planned activity where quiet is expected and the speaker is the focus of attention. The importance of poetry sharing to children is directly related to the teacher's enthusiasm and prominence he or she gives the art.

Choosing Poems

Choosing poetry to read to children is first dictated by a teacher's like or dislike of a poem. Poetry that is disliked intensely has no place in his or her repertoire. The desirability of a poem, and poetry itself, becomes apparent when children notice a flatness in the oral reading or a "sigh-like" shrug from the teacher which indicates "I'm doing this for your poetic enlightenment."

Initially, poetry for reading to children should come from established poets. Poetry having rhyme, rhythm, and humor captivates them and sets a pattern for more exciting reading sessions in the future. Shel Silverstein's, *Where the Sidewalk Ends*, and the humor section in any of the children's anthologies are excellent places to start. Then move on to all the other wonderful types of poetry that fill public and school library shelves.

Read poetry in short, enthusiastic bursts so children do not become bored. Then ask for volunteers to read their poetic writing or ask if you can read it for them. Poetic writing is a private matter and children should not be embarrassed by forced readings. Most children will respond, some hesitantly, as the poetic reading sessions continue with sensitive and vigorous readings of their works.

Reading Aloud

Before poetry is read aloud to a group, it should be read silently by the teacher or child. This is a time to note the poet's theme, underline vocabulary, find places to stress and emphasize, and locate places to pause. When possible, poetry should be read aloud as practice without an audience. A tape recorder gives excellent feedback at this point.

Although the reading of poetry and poetic writing should ring with enthusiasm, it should not be used as a display case of one's vocal abilities. The reader is subservient to the poem. The rhythm, intimacy, and meaning should highlight the reading.

Naturalness in delivery allows the poem to do its work. Most poems are meant for slow, deliberate reading, to be savored and enjoyed. A couplet three centuries old still holds a profound truth:

> Learn to read slow: All other graces
> Will follow in their proper places.
>
> *William Walker (1623–1684)*

Discussion sessions following the reading of poetry or poetic writing are important. This, too, is a time for savoring, not for deep, critical analysis. Let the critics do the analyzing; children should enjoy poetry and discuss why they enjoyed what they heard and, perhaps, hear it again. They should also have the option of going on to some other activity.

Memorizing

In the past children were encouraged, cajoled, and even threatened to "learn by heart" long, involved, and often, dull poems. Memorization of poetry still has its place but children should choose what they want to memorize. A poem, whether written by an established poet or yourself, must speak of your own experience and enlarge that experience.

The author did poetic writing in quatrain form soon after he started teaching in an elementary school. Four lines bob into his mind occasionally because of the vividness of certain individuals and the recurring nature of the problem. This is the type of poetic writing that stays in a person's mind and makes memorization easy.

> On viewing my attendance record,
> I find to my dismay,
> The children who are mischief makers
> Never miss a day.

Children and adults often know more poetry than they realize; Mother Goose rhymes, psalms, proverbs, and even the jingles from television commercials. Discussing these examples is one way to begin memorization sessions.

Normally, poetry and poetic writing selections chosen for memorization should be short; four lines at the most. Read them over several times in unison. If the rhythm dictates, have the children beat out the time with two fingers in the palms of their hands. Then emphasize particular words and the beat as you repeat the poem with them.

Repetition of the poem with the class can be done between changing classes, waiting in line for lunch, or going to lockers to get coats. There are many times during the day that can be utilized for poetry memorization.

Write more difficult poems and poetic writing on the chalkboard. Erase words randomly as the children read from the chalkboard aloud. After a few readings and erasures, many times a poem will sink into memory quite quickly.

What words do you remember from the following poem? Don't look back until you have tried to fill in the blanks.

On viewing _____ attendance _____ ,

I find to my _____ ,

The _____ who are _____ ,

Never _____ a _____ .

Choral Speaking

Choral speaking in this context is the group interpretation of poetry or poetic writing. Just as music is interpreted in many different ways by various conductors and musicians, so is poetry. Children can quickly learn to do this when given the opportunity to suggest their views. A poem that can be memorized in about three readings, "The Grand Old Duke of York," is an excellent example:

> The grand Old Duke of York
>   He had ten thousand men,
> He marched them up a very high hill
>   And marched them down again.
> And when he was up he was up,
>   And when he was down he was down.
> And when he was only half way up
>   He was neither up nor down.

Children will suggest marching, moving their bodies up and down at appropriate times, being expansive in their gestures with the word "grand," and numerous other ideas and activities.

Voice Groupings

After they have decided on various interpretations, divide the class by voice levels. In the primary grades two levels, low and high, are best. The intermediate and upper grades can be divided into low, middle, and high voices.

The simplest way to determine voice levels is to have individual children count in a normal voice to five. You and the class then decide on what level to classify each person. Sometimes comparisons need to be made by having two children count out loud, one immediately after the other. Children are amazed to hear such differences in the pitches of their voices.

Since they know "The Grand Old Duke of York," the next step is to place the groups in different parts of the room and assign each their lines.

Generally, the medium voices introduce choral readings. High level voices often have lines with more "s" sounds and appropriate wording. The low level voices have the more guttural sounds and somber moods and meanings. Here is one way to divide "The Grand Old Duke of York."

Medium	The grand Old Duke of York
	He had ten thousand men,
High	He marched them up a very high hill
Low	And marched them down again.
High	And when he was up he was up
Low	And when he was down he was down.
Medium	And when he was only halfway up
	He was neither
High	up
Medium	nor
Low	down.

> See
> Appendix
> Item
> 47

If you have not done choral speaking before, try doing "The Grand Old Duke of York" and some other favorite poems such as "The Chickens" and "Poor Old Woman." Then move on to the children's poetic writing as choral speaking.

> See
> Appendix
> Item
> 48, 49

Poetic Writing Oral Interpretation

Poetic writing lends itself to various forms of creative oral expression. Solos, group responses, speaking in unison, and physical movement are all possible.

Ask several children to stand across the front of the classroom. Assign each a line from an address poem as in the one below. Those with numbers will form themselves into the appropriate numbers; those with letters will become letters. As they say their lines in rapid fire fashion, have them determine just the right amount of expression.

See
Appendix
Item
17

Poem: 7155 S.W. 93 St.

7	I'm not a fabricator,
1	nor
5	prevaricator,
5	nor a perjuror.
S.	So
W.	when
9	*I* concoct an incredible tale,
3	I am a
S	story-
t.	teller.

Name poems lend themselves to solo and group interpretation of poetic writing. For example:

R	reasonable	spoken in a *reasonable* tone of voice and manner
U	useful	spoken with dramatic emphasis on *ful*
T	terrific	spoken with rolling *r*'s and rolling eyes
H	helpful	spoken with hands and arms outstretched

See
Appendix
Item
21

See
Appendix
Item
24

Two-word poems also lend themselves to various oral and physical interpretations of the words.

My father	spoken matter-of-factly
Strong arms	spoken gruffly with biceps flexed
Thin face	spoken with hands drawn across face

Definite opinions	spoken with right arm cocked and finger pointed in an accusatory manner
Hard worker	spoken with emphasis on hand and body in a strained lifting position
Family man	spoken with arms enveloping imaginary family

Children's poetic writing of haiku, tanka, cinquain, and other oriental types of poems are enhanced with musical background. The oral interpretations might include sound effects of weather and various oral emphasis on words such as those found in the action and feeling lines of the cinquain.

Ways to Share Orally

Poetic writing can be shared orally in many ways. Here are a few that may serve as reminders to those who have used them in the past or, perhaps, spark new techniques for sharing in the future.

- Tape record on reel to reel or cassette tapes children's poetic writing and place the tapes in a "Poetic Writing Interest Center" or send them home for parents to listen to.

- Ask the principal to allow time during morning announcements for children to read a few of their poetic writings over the public address system.

- Put choral speaking of poetic writing on the school videotape machine for viewing and listening by other classes.

- Prepare an assembly for choral speaking of poetic writing.

- Have a "Share Your Best" session with classes on the same grade levels. Let the children choose several of their peers to go to another class to share their poetic writing. The other classes then reciprocate.

- Organize an after school or late afternoon Poetic Writing Club or Poetry Club of five or six children. Allow the children to set rules for membership and share their poetic writing with each other.

WRITTEN SHARING

When children are ready to share their poetic writing, the written message should be as perfect as they can make it. This is the time to correct spelling errors, put punctuation marks in their proper places, and write as legibly as possible. Material that is to be read by others is a mirrored reflection of the author's abilities—or lack of abilities. Children should be taught to be diligent proofreaders.

Booklets

Duplicating machines have simplified the process of developing multiple copies of written material quickly. Ditto or spirit master sheets can be made by children. They not only can print or type their own poetic writing on a spirit master but also do illustrations. After running off the pages desired, it is a simple matter to staple the material together and add a colorful construction paper cover and back page.

Mimeographed stencils are more difficult to work with. A school secretary or perhaps an interested parent with good typing skills can make a stencil. Mimeographed pages have the advantages of legibility and being able to provide more copies per stencil than spirit masters. Some schools even have this material bound with photographs on the covers.

See
Appendix
Item
50

Transparencies with an Overhead Projector

Shorter poetic writing such as the haiku is easily printed on acetates with water soluble felt pens and shown on a wall, screen, or even the chalkboard with an overhead projector. The children can read and discuss the writing as a group. If changes are desired, wipe a damp tissue or cloth over the acetate to clean off the printing and allow for any changes.

Transparencies with poetry and poetic writing are useful when a total class must read together. The poetry in the Appendix can be made into transparencies by running a page with an infrared transparency film through a thermal heat unit. The printing is embossed permanently on the transparency. See your audiovisual specialist for details if you are not familiar with this process.

Opaque Projector

An opaque projector requires a completely darkened room but offers children a quick way of sharing their poetic writing with the total class. The papers they write and illustrate can be shown immediately and directly on a wall, screen, or chalkboard for all to read.

Bulletin Boards

Classroom bulletin boards are the traditional place to show off children's writing.* It is important that children are recognized for their accomplishments. The bulletin board should highlight their work in the best manner possible. By placing the children's names in black letters on two-inch cards under their works, everyone, including themselves, can see their names and materials from any point in the room. By simply folding the outer edges of the children's papers, as shown in the illustration, their poetic writing will be highlighted also.

Newspapers

Most classrooms at some time or another publish their own newspaper.† They range from the simple spirit master type to those printed on newsprint. The various kinds of poetic writing children do should find a place in the classroom newspaper for others to read. A "Poetry Column" is just as appropriate as a sports or gossip column.

Children's Magazines

There are numerous children's magazines that publish the writing of young people.‡ Before sending any material to these magazines be sure to read the magazines first and follow the directions explicitly for submitting material.

Commercial Magazines

Below is a partial list of children's magazines you could send material to. Your school or public library probably subscribes to these and many others. *Read the magazines first before sending children's writing.* Magazine requirements often change quickly.

*See Arnold B. Cheyney, *The Writing Corner*, Chapter Three, "Creating Atmosphere for Writing" (Santa Monica, Calif.: Goodyear, 1979).

†See Arnold B. Cheyney, *The Writing Corner*, Chapter Seven, "Creating a Classroom Newspaper" (Santa Monica, Calif.: Goodyear, 1979).

‡See Kathleen Copeland, "Sharing Your Students: Where and How to Publish Children's Work," *Language Arts* 57 (September 1980), 635–648.

Child Life
P.O. Box 567B
Indianapolis, IN 46206

Children's Playmate
P.O. Box 567B
Indianapolis, IN 46206

Jack and Jill
P.O. Box 567B
Indianapolis, IN 46206

Cricket
P.O. Box 100
LaSalle, IL 61301

Dynamite
50 West 44th Street
New York, NY 10036

Daisy
830 Third Avenue
New York, NY 10022

Ebony, Jr.!
820 S. Michigan Avenue
Chicago, IL 60605

The Electric Company Magazine
P.O. Box 2926
Boulder, CO 80322

Highlights for Children
803 Church Street
Honesdale, PA 18431

Stone Soup
P.O. Box 83
Santa Cruz, CA 95063

Denominational Magazines

There are hundreds of denominational school programs that publish literature for children for use in Saturday and Sunday classes. They cover the broad religious spectrum of Protestant, Catholic, and Jewish religious groups and include other unaffiliated or independent organizations. Encourage those children who do attend weekend services to read their literature carefully to determine if their church or organization solicits children's material through their publications. A great many do. *The Writer's Market*, published annually (9933 Alliance Road, Cincinnati, OH 45424, or available at your public library) lists many denominational and commercial magazines under Juvenile, and Teen and Young Adult classifications.

THE POETRY CORNER

Many classrooms have various types of interest centers—a place where children may go to pursue an activity of their choice when they complete their regular classroom studies. Just having an interest center in a quiet area of the classroom devoted to poetic writing can fix in children's minds the importance poetic writing holds in a teacher's scheme of the best curriculum. A poetry corner deserves equal space with science, reading, and social studies interest areas. All of these disciplines contribute to each other in developing the intellect and personalities of children.

Materials

A poetry corner needs materials that are readily available to the children when they sit down to write.* These items should include:

pencils

erasers

writing paper

books of poetry

children's magazines

dictionaries

rhyming dictionary

word lists

construction paper

stapler

crayons

felt pens

acetates

infrared transparency film

water soluble felt pens

tissues or cloths

duplicated Appendix pages from *The Poetry Corner*

One ought,
everyday at least,
to hear a little song,
read a good poem,
see a fine picture, and,
if it were possible,
to speak a few reasonable words.

Johann Wolfgang Von Goethe (1749–1832)

*See Dolores G. Gonzales, "An Author Center for Children," *Language Arts* 57 (March 1980) 280–284.

BIBLIOGRAPHIES

PUBLISHED POETRY OF CHILDREN

Baron, Virginia Olson, ed. *Here I Am! An Anthology of Poems Written by Young People in Some of America's Minority Groups.* New York: Bantam Books, 1969.

Grosvenor, Kali. *Poems by Kali.* Garden City, N.Y.: Doubleday, 1970. (Poems by an eight-year-old girl)

Hopkins, Lee Bennett, ed. *City Talk.* New York: Alfred A. Knopf, 1970. (Cinquain poetry)

Jordon, June and Bush, Terri, eds. *The Voice of the Children.* New York: Washington Square Press, 1974.

Larrick, Nancy, ed. *I Heard a Scream in the Night: Poems by Young People in the City.* New York: Dell, 1970.

Lewis, Richard, ed. *Miracles: Poems by Children of the English-Speaking World.* New York: Simon & Schuster, 1966.

Mendoza, George, ed. *The World from My Window.* New York: Hawthorn Books, 1969.

Volavková, Hana, ed. *I Never Saw Another Butterfly: Children's Drawings and Poems from Terezin Concentration Camp, 1942–1944.* Translated by Jeanne Něcomcavá. New York: McGraw-Hill, 1962.

POETRY BOOKS FOR CHILDREN

Adams, Adriene, *Poetry of Earth.* New York: Charles Scribner's Sons, 1972.

Aldis, Dorothy. *All Together: A Child's Treasury of Verse.* New York: G.P. Putnam's Sons, 1952.

——. *Is Anybody Hungry?* New York: G.P. Putnam's Sons, 1964.

de Angeli, Marguerite. *Marguerite de Angeli's A Pocket Full of Posies: A Merry Mother Goose.* Garden City, N.Y.: Doubleday, 1961.

Asch, Frank. *City Sandwich.* New York: William Morrow, 1978.

Atwood, Ann. *Haiku: The Mood of Earth.* New York: Charles Scribner's Sons, 1971.

Benét, Stephen Vincent. *The Ballad of William Sycamore (1790–1871).* Boston: Little, Brown, 1959.

Blishen, Edward, ed. *Oxford Book of Poetry for Children.* New York: Franklin Watts, 1963.

Bontemps, Arna, ed. *American Negro Poetry.* New York: Hill and Wang, 1963.

Brian Wildsmith's Mother Goose: A Collection of Nursery Rhymes. New York: Franklin Watts, 1964.

Brown, Margaret Wise. *Nibble Nibble: Poems for Children.* New York: Young Scott Books, 1959.

Clithero, Sally, ed. *Beginning to Read Poetry: Selected from Original Sources.* Chicago: Follett, 1967.

Ciardi, John. *I Met a Man.* Boston: Houghton Mifflin, 1961.

——. *The Reason for the Pelican.* Philadelphia: J.B. Lippincott, 1959.

Daugherty, James. *West of Boston: Yankee Rhymes and Doggerel.* New York: Viking, 1956.

Dickinson, Emily. *I'm Nobody! Who Are You? Poems of Emily Dickinson for Children.* Owings Mills, MD.: Stemmer House, 1978.

Dunbar, Paul Laurence. *I Greet the Dawn.* New York: Atheneum, 1978.

Dunning, Stephen; Lueders, Edward; and Smith, Hugh, eds. *Reflections on a Gift of Watermelon Pickle: And Other Modern Verse.* New York: Lothrop, Lee & Shepard Co., 1967.

——. *Some Haystacks Don't Even Have Any Needle: And Other Complete Modern Poems.* Glenview, IL.: Scott, Foresman and Company, 1969.

Frost, Robert. *Stopping by Woods on a Snowy Evening*. New York: E.P. Dutton (Illustrations copyright Susan Jeffers), 1978.

Giovanni, Nikki. *Ego-tripping and Other Poems for Young People*. New York: Lawrence Hill and Company, 1973.

Greenfield, Eloise. *Honey, I Love: And Other Love Poems*. New York: Thomas Y. Crowell, 1972.

Hoberman, Mary Ann. *Bugs*. New York: Viking, 1976.

Hopkins, Lee Bennett, ed. *The City Spreads Its Wings*. New York: Franklin Watts, 1970.

Hughes, Langston. *Don't You Turn Back*. New York: Alfred A. Knopf, 1969.

Jordon, June, ed. *Soulscript: Afro-American Poetry*. New York: Zenith Books, 1970.

Larrick, Nancy, ed. *On City Streets: An Anthology of Poetry*. New York: M. Evans and Company, 1968.

——. *Piping Down the Valleys Wild*. New York: Dell, 1968

——. *Poetry for Holidays*. Champaign, IL: Garrard Publishing Company, 1966.

Lewis, C. Day. *Poetry for You: A Book for Boys and Girls on the Enjoyment of Poetry*. Oxford, England: Basil Blackwell, 1961.

Livingston, Myra Cohn, ed. *O Frabjous Day! Poetry for Holidays and Special Occasions*. New York: Atheneum, 1977.

McCord, David. *Every Time I Climb a Tree*. Boston: Little, Brown, 1967.

——. *Far and Few: Rhymes of the Never Was and Always Is*. Boston: Little, Brown, 1952.

——. *One at a Time: His Collected Poems for the Young*. Boston: Little, Brown, 1974.

——. *Take Sky: More Rhymes of the Never Was and Always Is*. Boston: Little, Brown, 1962.

Merriam, Eve. *Catch a Little Rhyme*. New York: Atheneum, 1967.

——. *It Doesn't Have to Rhyme*. New York: Atheneum, 1975.

——. *There Is No Rhyme for Silver*. New York: Atheneum, 1962.

Moore, Lillian, ed. *Go With the Poem*. New York: McGraw-Hill, 1979.

Nash, Ogden. *The New Nutcracker Suite and Other Innocent Verses*. Boston: Little, Brown, 1962.

O'Neill, Mary. *Hailstones and Halibut Bones: Adventures in Color*. Garden City, N.Y.: Doubleday, 1961.

——. *Take a Number*. Garden City, N.Y.: Doubleday, 1968.

——. *Winds*. Garden City, N.Y.: Doubleday, 1970.

Plotz, Helen, ed. *The Gift Outright: America to Her Poets*. New York: Greenwillow Books, 1977.

Prelutsky, Jack. *A Gopher in the Garden: And Other Animal Poems*. New York: Macmillan, 1967.

——. *Nightmares: Poems to Trouble Your Sleep*. New York: Greenwillow Books, 1976.

——. *The Snopp on the Sidewalk: And Other Poems*. New York: Greenwillow Books, 1977.

——. *Toucans Two: And Other Poems*. New York: Macmillan, 1970.

Reed, Gwendolyn, ed. *Out of the Ark: An Anthology of Animal Verse*. New York: Atheneum, 1968.

de Regniers, Beatrice Schenk; Moore, Eva; and White, Mary Michaels. *Poems Children Will Sit Still For: A Selection for the Primary Grades*. New York: Citation Press, 1969.

Schwartz, Alvin, ed. *A Twister of Twists, A Tangler of Tongues*. Philadelphia: J.B. Lippincott, 1972.

Service, Robert W. *The Shooting of Dan McGrew: The Cremation of Sam McGee*. New York: Young Scott Books, 1969.

Silverstein, Shel. *Where the Sidewalk Ends*. New York: Harper & Row, 1974.

Snyder, Zilpha Keatley. *Today Is Saturday*. New York: Atheneum, 1969.

Thayer, Ernest Lawrence. *Casey at the Bat*. Englewood Cliffs, N.J.: Prentice-Hall, 1964.

Turman, Judith. *Flashlight: And Other Poems*. New York: Atheneum, 1976.

Weiss, Renée Karol. *A Paper Zoo: A Collection of Animal Poems by Modern American Poets*. New York: Macmillan, 1968.

Whitman, Walt. *Overhead the Sun: Lines from Walt Whitman*. New York: Farrar, Straus and Giroux (woodcuts copyright Antonio Frasconi), 1969.

Whittier, John Greenleaf. *Barbara Frietchie*. New York: Thomas Y. Crowell (illustrations copyright Paul Galdone), 1965.

Withers, Carl, ed. *A Rocket in My Pocket: The Rhymes and Chants of Young Americans*. New York: Holt, Rinehart and Winston, 1948.

Zolotow, Charlotte. *River Winding*. New York: Thomas Y. Crowell, 1970.

POETRY REFERENCE BOOKS FOR TEACHERS

Arbuthnot, May Hill and Broderick, Dorothy M. Revised by Zena Sutherland. *The Arbuthnot Anthology of Children's Literature*. Glenview, IL.: Scott, Foresman and Company, 1976.

Arnstein, Flora J. *Poetry in the Elementary Classroom*. New York: Appleton-Century-Crofts, 1962.

Boyd, Gertrude, A. *Teaching Poetry in the Elementary School*. Columbus, OH.: Charles E. Merrill, 1973.

Butscher, Edward. *Adelaide Crapsey*. Boston: Twayne Publishing, 1979.

Carlson, Ruth Kearney. *Poetry for Today's Child*. Dansville, N.Y.: The Instructor Publications, Inc., 1968.

——. *Writing Aids through the Grades: One Hundred Eighty-six Developmental Writing Activities*. New York: Teachers College Press, 1970.

Chukovsky, Komei, *From Two to Five*. Translated and edited by Miriam Morton. Berkeley: University of California Press, 1963.

Gensler, Kinereth and Nyhart, Nina. *The Poetry Connection: An Anthology of Contemporary Poems with Ideas to Stimulate Children's Writing*. New York: Teachers & Writers, 1978.

Glaus, Marlene. *From Thoughts to Words*. Urbana, IL.: National Council of Teachers of English, 1965.

Henderson, Harold G. *Haiku in English*. Rutland, VT.: Charles E. Tuttle Company, 1967.

——. An Introduction to Haiku: *An Anthology of Poems and Poets from Bashō to Shiki*. Garden City, N.Y.: Doubleday, 1958.

Hopkins, Lee Bennett. *Pass the Poetry, Please! Using Poetry in Pre-Kindergarten–Six Classrooms*. New York: Citation Press, 1972.

Johnson, Edna, et. al. *Anthology of Children's Literature*. 5th ed. Boston: Houghton Mifflin, 1977.

Kaminsky, Marc. *What's Inside You It Shines Out of You*. New York: Horizon Press, 1974.

Kimzey, Arids. *To Defend a Form: The Romance of Administration and Teaching in a Poetry-in-the-Schools Program*. New York: Teachers & Writers, 1977.

Koch, Kenneth. *Rose, Where Did You Get That Red? Teaching Great Poetry to Children*. New York: Vintage Books, 1973.

Koch, Kenneth and the Students of P. S. 61 in New York City. *Wishes, Lies, and Dreams: Teaching Children to Write Poetry*. New York: Chelsea House Publishers, 1970.

Purves, Alan C., ed. *How Porcupines Make Love: Notes on a Response-Centered Curriculum*. New York: John Wiley and Sons, 1977.

Riccio, Ottone M. *The Intimate Art of Writing Poetry*. Englewood Cliffs, N.J.: Prentice-Hall, 1980.

Terry, Ann. *Children's Poetry Preferences: A National Survey of Upper Elementary Grades*. Urbana, IL: National Council of Teachers of English, 1972.

Ullyette, Jean M. *Guidelines for Creative Writing*. Dansville, N.Y.: The Instructor Publications, Inc., 1968.

Whitman, Ruth and Feinberg, Harriet, eds. *Poemmaking: Poets in the Classroom*. Lawrence, MA: Massachusetts Council of Teachers of English, 1975.

Williams, Emmett, ed. *An Anthology of Concrete Poetry*. New York: Something Else Press, 1967.

Witucke, Virginia. *Poetry in the Elementary School*. Dubuque, IA: William C. Brown Company, 1970.

Wolsch, Robert A. *Poetic Composition Through the Grades: A Language Sensitivity Program*. New York: Teachers College Press, 1970.

APPENDIX

Ready-to-duplicate materials
to individualize poetic writing

Convert each page to a duplicating
master in a master-making unit.
Reproduce copies for classroom use only.

APPENDIX ITEM 1

TOUCHING

Write about the *touching* you see in the pictures.

From *The Poetry Corner* by Arnold Cheyney © 1982 Scott, Foresman and Company.

APPENDIX ITEM 2

TASTING

Write about the *tasting* you see in the pictures.

_____

_____

_____

_____

_____

_____

_____

_____

_____

_____

_____

_____

APPENDIX ITEM 3

SMELLING

Write about the *smells* you see in the pictures.

_____

_____

_____

_____

_____

_____

_____

_____

_____

_____

_____

_____

_____

_____

_____

APPENDIX ITEM 4

SEEING

Write about what you *see* in the pictures.

_____

_____

_____

_____

_____

_____

_____

_____

_____

_____

_____

_____

From *The Poetry Corner* by Arnold Cheyney © 1982 Scott, Foresman and Company.

APPENDIX ITEM 5

HEARING

Write about what you *hear* in the pictures.

APPENDIX ITEM 6

SIMILES

The simile is a comparison of things that are not alike. A writer uses words such as *like* or *as*. For example, William Wordsworth wrote:

Thy soul was like a star, and dwelt apart,

Thou hadst a voice whose sound was like the sea. . . .

Now try making your own similes. The illustrations on either side of the paper will give you an idea of what you might write in the blanks.

From *The Poetry Corner* by Arnold Cheyney © 1982 Scott, Foresman and Company.

   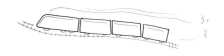

_____ like _____

_____ as _____

   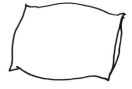

_____

_____

APPENDIX ITEM 7

METAPHORS

The metaphor suggests that there is a comparison to be made between one object and another although the objects are quite different. Connecting words such as *like* or *as* are not used in the metaphor. A master of the metaphor was William Shakespeare:

OBJECT   =   OBJECT

It is the east and *Juliet* is the *sun*.

OBJECTS   =

All the world's a stage, and all the *men* and *women*

     OBJECT

merely *players*.

Now, try making your own metaphors. The illustrations on either side of the page will give you some idea of what to write in the blanks.

_____ is _____

_____ is _____

_____

_____

APPENDIX ITEM 8

I USED TO/BUT NOW

Do you remember what you thought about when you were small? Perhaps you wanted to be an astronaut, but now you want to be a Marine. Or, you may have lived in Minnesota but now you live in North Carolina. Here's how to use your memory to write these poems.

I used to dream of being an astronaut
But now I want to be a United States Marine.

I used to live in Minnesota
But now I live in North Carolina.

Now, try doing some on your own. Use the pictures to start you thinking if you wish.

I used to _____

But now _____

I used to _____

But now _____

I used to _____

But now _____

I used to _____

But now _____

From *The Poetry Corner* by Arnold Cheyney © 1982 Scott, Foresman and Company.

APPENDIX ITEM 9

LIE POEMS

In poetic writing you don't have to tell the truth; you may lie. For example:

 I used to like ice cream
But now I eat only spinach.

I used to be a frog
But now I'm a praying mantis.

Now, you try some. Use the illustrations to get started if you wish.

 I used to _____

_____

But now _____

_____

I used to _____

But now _____

_____

I used to _____

_____

But now _____

_____

I used to _____

But now _____

_____

APPENDIX ITEM 10

I AM/BUT I WISH I WERE

All of us at some time or another wish we were somebody else. In this poem you can be whatever or whomever you wish. For example:

I am a girl
But I wish I were a famous movie star receiving an Oscar!

I am a boy
But I wish I were a pro football star running for a touchdown on the last play of the game to win the Super Bowl!

Now, you try. Be what you want or let the illustrations help you.

I am _____

_____

But I wish I were _____

_____

I am _____

_____

But I wish I were _____

_____

I am _____

_____

But I wish I were _____

_____

I am _____

_____

But I wish I were _____

_____

APPENDIX ITEM 11

ALLITERATION

Alliteration surrounds us. An advertisement shouts: Big Bonus! Super Savings Special! Alliteration is generally found in the beginning sounds of words but it is also heard in the middle and ends of words in a series. See how many you can find in a newspaper or magazine, cut them out, and paste them below. At the bottom of the page write some of your own.

From *The Poetry Corner* by Arnold Cheyney © 1982 Scott, Foresman and Company.

APPENDIX ITEM 12

FREE VERSE

Free verse is written material freed from paragraph form. There is no rhyme but there is rhythm. Free verse flows along easily because it is broken up on the page in words, phrases, and sentences. For example, Lincoln's "Address at Gettysburg" is rearranged in free verse to make it easier to read and speak. Try doing the same thing with some of your own writing.

Fourscore and seven years
ago our fathers brought
forth on this continent, a
new nation, conceived in
Liberty, and dedicated to
the proposition that all men
are created equal.

Fourscore and seven years ago
our fathers brought forth
on this continent
a new nation,
conceived in Liberty,
and dedicated to the proposition
that
all men are created equal.

From *The Poetry Corner* by Arnold Cheyney © 1982 Scott, Foresman and Company.

APPENDIX ITEM 13

CONCRETE POETRY — BOY

Concrete poetry, also called picture poetry, is formed to look like what your are writing about. A poem about a snowman is in the shape of a snowman; a poem about rain is in the shape of an umbrella.

Cut out the head of a boy on this page. Discard the center piece and place the outline over another sheet of paper. Write or type words, phrases, or sentences about the boy within the section removed. Lift off the pattern when finished and you will have your own concrete poem.

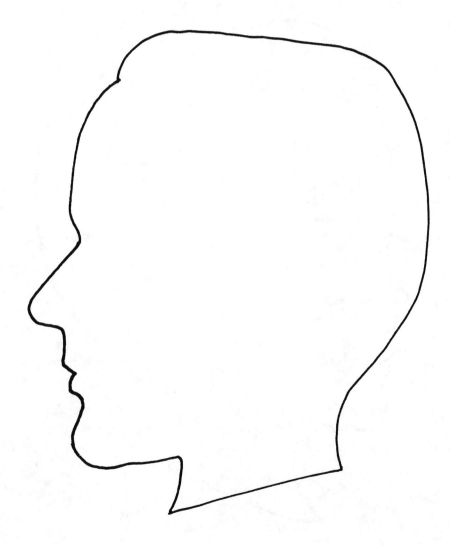

APPENDIX ITEM 14

CONCRETE POETRY — GIRL

Concrete poetry, also called picture poetry, is formed to look like what you are writing about. A poem about a flower is in the shape of a flower; a poem about a kite is in the shape of a kite.

Cut out the head of a girl on this page. Discard the center piece and place the outline over another sheet of paper. Write or type words, phrases, or sentences about the girl within the section removed. Lift off the pattern when finished and you will have your own concrete poem.

From *The Poetry Corner* by Arnold Cheyney © 1982 Scott, Foresman and Company.

APPENDIX ITEM 15

CONCRETE POETRY — THE ZOO

Write yourself around the zoo. You will visit a tiger, elephant, giraffe, bear, rhinoceros, and lion. Turn your paper as you write. You can write one line from the time you ENTER until you EXIT or short poems at each cage.

APPENDIX ITEM 16

LICENSE PLATE POEMS

There is poetic writing in the numbers and letters of a license plate. Write the license plate numbers and letters in a vertical column. After each letter write a word that begins with that letter. After each number write a word or words containing the number of syllables or that number of words. Here's one in letters and syllables.

N 43933 D

N	Notice!
4	Your permission
3	to drive is
9	temporarily suspended till
3	age 60.
3	Cordially,
D	Dad

APPENDIX ITEM 17

ADDRESS POEMS

Your address can tell more than where you live. As poetic writing it contains a message about you for others to read. Write your address on the line, then copy it vertically down the side of the paper. For every number write a word or words containing that number of syllables. For every letter, write a word beginning with that letter.

My address: _____

From *The Poetry Corner* by Arnold Cheyney © 1982 Scott, Foresman and Company.

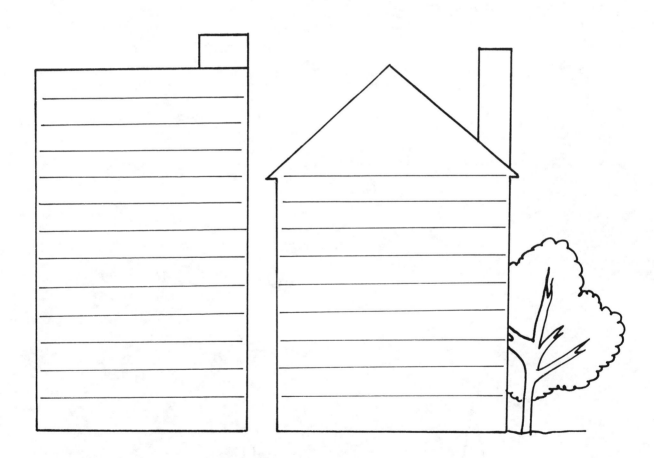

APPENDIX ITEM 18

CITY, STATE POEMS

What words come to your mind when you think of your city, town, or state?

Write the name of your city and state in column form below. Then write words after the letters that describe the places and also begin with the letters.

From *The Poetry Corner* by Arnold Cheyney © 1982 Scott, Foresman and Company.

APPENDIX ITEM 19

VERB POEMS

Verbs are useful. Some are used to show action that is occurring. The word *look,* for instance, may look right at you.

look

And "stepping" could go right off the page.

Try some.

```
                                    s
                                       t
                                         e
                                           p
                                             p
                                               i
                                                 n
jumping                                            g
```

steaming

falling

growing

eating

APPENDIX ITEM 20

NOUN POEMS

Among the things that a noun does is to give names to persons, places, conditions, and things. The letters of the nouns can't look like the things they represent, but with a little imagination they can. For example, the letters in airplane can look like an airplane.

airplane

The word slump looks like this, poetically speaking, of course.

S   P
  L   M
   U

What can you do with these words?

dump   automobile

tree   fish

fire engine   cup

APPENDIX ITEM 21

NAME POEMS

How do you want your friends to think of you? As energetic, terrific, handsome, beautiful, intelligent?

If so, write a poem about yourself and start to believe it. Write your name vertically. Use words beginning with the letters in your name that are the *you* you want people to see and know. If your name were DON, you might write:

> DON
>
> D Dashing
> O Organized
> N Neat

Now, you try it!

_____ _____

_____ _____

_____ _____

_____ _____

_____ _____

_____ _____

_____ _____

_____ _____

_____ _____

APPENDIX ITEM 22

NEWSPAPER POEMS — HEADLINES

To do this poem you will need an old newspaper, scissors, paste, and paper. Cut out a number of headlines and words that interest you from the newspaper. Rearrange them until you have a poem.

You don't have to be **perfect** to be part of the **ADULT EXERCISE CLASS** you can **TAKE OFF 25%.**

From *The Poetry Corner* by Arnold Cheyney © 1982 Scott, Foresman and Company.

APPENDIX ITEM 23

NEWSPAPER POEMS—PARAGRAPHS

The newspaper has more poetic writing in it than you may think. Cut out paragraphs of interesting writing. Then underline words, phrases, and sentences that catch your eye and arrange them into your poetic writing.

NOT LISTENING

People told me
I'd never make it.
That was real incentive.

People told me
I'd never make it.
They were wrong.

A real small town,
Not many players.
They were wrong.

"I come out of a real small town," he says, "and not many football players have come from there. There were a lot of people who told me I'd never make it. That was a real incentive for me. I wanted to show people they were wrong."

APPENDIX ITEM 24

TWO-WORD POEMS

Two-word poems are limited to two words per line. There is no rhyming. An easy way to begin is to start with a subject such as a person, animal, or thing. Describe the subject in two-word lines until you are finished. For instance, if you had a pet boa constrictor, you might write:

Boa constrictor
Large snake
Eats mice
Glides along
Very large
My friend
Guards house
No problems
Know why?

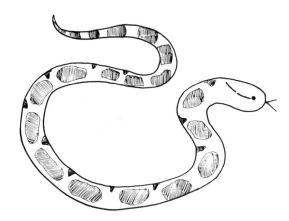

APPENDIX ITEM 25

HAIKU

    The *haiku* (HIGH-koo) is a Japanese unrhymed poem about nature and the seasons of the year. It has three lines and totals seventeen syllables. The first line has five syllables, the second line seven syllables, and the third line five syllables. You do not have to follow the syllable count exactly but you should use a word that hints of the season of the year as you write these nature poems. Make the event in your poem happen in the present.

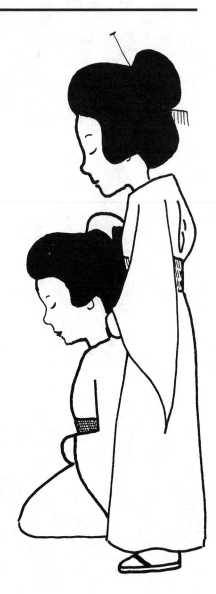

5 _____

7 _____

5 _____

5 _____

7 _____

5 _____

APPENDIX ITEM 26

TANKA

The *tanka* is a haiku with two additional lines of seven syllables each. The tankas are also about nature and a season of the year. In the tanka the first three lines are called hokku, the last two lines are called ageku.

5 _____   5 _____

7 _____   7 _____

5 _____   5 _____

7 _____   7 _____

7 _____   7 _____

5 _____   5 _____

7 _____   7 _____

5 _____   5 _____

7 _____   7 _____

7 _____   7 _____

APPENDIX ITEM 27

RENGA

The *renga* is a Japanese poem where several persons write the poem. The first part, a haiku (5,7,5), is written by one person, another person does the next two lines (7,7), another writes the next part (5,7,5), another does two lines (7,7), and so on. The same theme should run through the renga. Get together with four or five other students who are interested and do several at one time.

5 _____

7 _____

5 _____

7 _____

7 _____

5 _____

7 _____

5 _____

7 _____

7 _____

5 _____

7 _____

5 _____

7 _____

7 _____

5 _____

7 _____

5 _____

7 _____

7 _____

APPENDIX ITEM 28

SENRYU

The *senryu* is in haiku form, that is, three lines with syllables of 5, 7, 5. The senryu is different in that it is generally not about nature or the seasons of the year. A senryu can be about your favorite sports, hobbies, friends, relatives, foods, or whatever comes to your mind.

花
友 色

5 _____
7 _____
5 _____

5 _____
7 _____
5 _____

5 _____
7 _____
5 _____

5 _____
7 _____
5 _____

5 _____
7 _____
5 _____

5 _____
7 _____
5 _____

From *The Poetry Corner* by Arnold Cheyney © 1982 Scott, Foresman and Company.

APPENDIX ITEM 29

LANTERNE

The *lanterne* is a five-line, syllabic poem that ends up looking like a Japanese lantern.

Syllables	*Lanterne*
1	My
2	black cat,
3	back upraised,
4	tail tall. My dog,
1	gone!

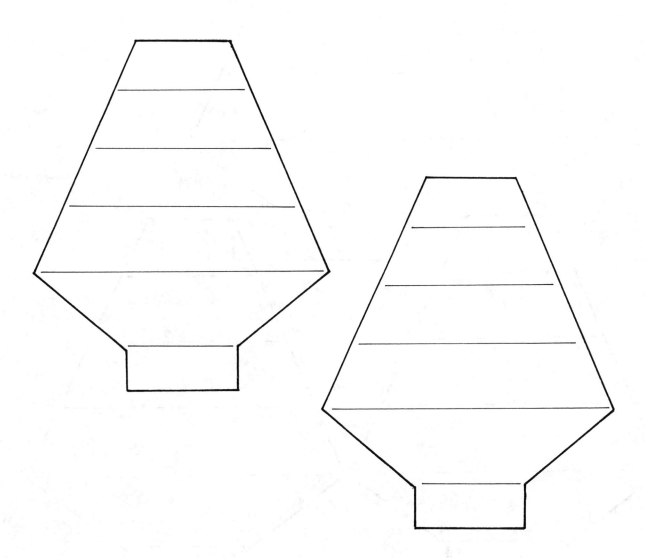

APPENDIX ITEM 30

CHAIN LANTERNE

The *chain lanterne* is made up of several lanterne poems. One person can write them or several can write them together. Be sure to keep the same theme or subject.

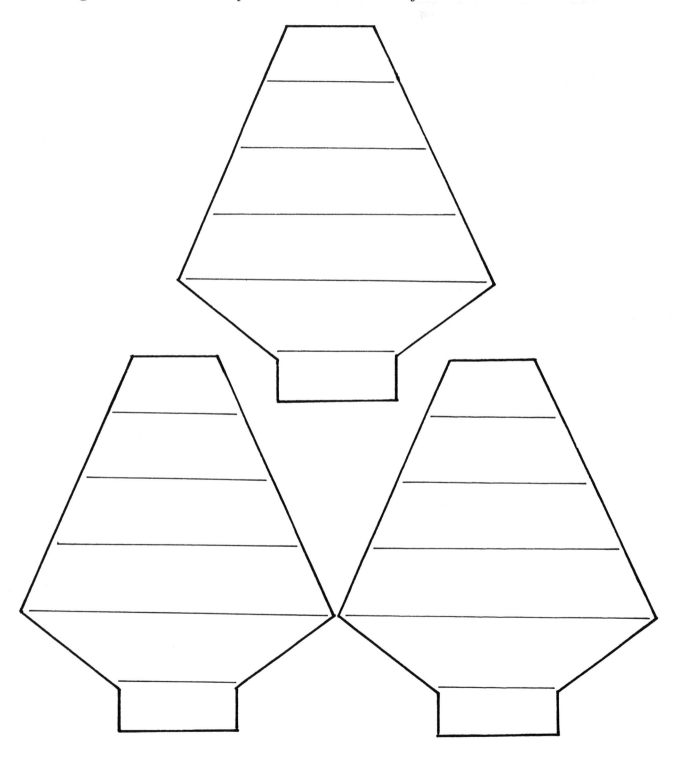

APPENDIX ITEM 31

CINQUAIN

The *cinquain* (SIN-kane) is a five-line poem. Each line has a set number of syllables and each line must tell something specific about the title.

SYLLABLES	DESCRIPTION	EXAMPLE
2	title	Flowers
4	description of title	Yellow, dark red
6	action	Waving in the morning
8	feeling	Their fragrance brings me happiness
2	another word for the title	Roses

APPENDIX ITEM 32

CHAIN CINQUAIN

The *chain cinquain* is a series of cinquains written by one person or several on the same theme or subject without following the specific description for each line. They make interesting notes and letters, too. Try writing one to a friend.

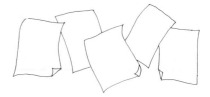

_____

_____

_____

_____

_____

_____

_____

_____

_____

_____

_____

_____

_____

_____

APPENDIX ITEM 33

DOUBLE CINQUAIN

A *double cinquain* is a cinquain with the syllables increased in each line. You need not keep to the descriptions for each line as in a cinquain.

SYLLABLES	EXAMPLE
4	Oak tree, gnarled trunk
8	Clutching earth, reaching for the sun.
12	You have been here since Indians have passed your feet.
16	Watching men divide earth and grasp for footholds in highest heaven.
4	What thoughts you have.

4 _____

8 _____

12 _____

16 _____

4 _____

From *The Poetry Corner* by Arnold Cheyney © 1982 Scott, Foresman and Company.

APPENDIX ITEM 34

DIAMANTE

The diamante (dee-ah-MAHN-tay) is a poem of opposites. The seven lines have the following requirements:

LINE

1 one-word subject: noun, opposite of word in last line
2 two words: adjectives describing subject in first line
3 three words: participles: *-ing, -ed* words about subject in first line
4 four words: nouns about subject in first and last lines
5 three words: participles: *-ing, -ed* words about subject in last line
6 two words: adjectives describing subject in last line
7 one-word subject: noun, opposite of word in first line

winter
cold, icy
snowing, frosting, freezing
frigidity, snowball, warmth, bonfire
broiling, scorching, sizzling
hot, warm
summer

Here are two starters for you.

noon   friend

_____   _____

_____   _____

_____   _____

_____   _____

midnight   foe

From *The Poetry Corner* by Arnold Cheyney © 1982 Scott, Foresman and Company.

APPENDIX ITEM 35

ANTONYMS

all	none	low	high
answer	ignore	many	few
appreciative	ungrateful	near	far
backward	forward	new	old
big	little	night	day
boy	girl	noisy	quiet
busy	idle	noon	midnight
calm	excited	north	south
clean	dirty	open	close
clear	hazy	past	future
combine	separate	personal	public
courageous	timid	positive	negative
cover	reveal	pretty	ugly
coward	hero	push	pull
dry	wet	short	tall
fast	slow	shy	outgoing
fat	thin	smart	dumb
friend	foe	stop	go
full	empty	straight	curved
funny	serious	sunny	cloudy
good	bad	sweet	sour
happy	sad	top	bottom
hard	soft	up	down
harm	protect	whisper	shout
hello	goodbye	win	lose
hot	cold	yes	no
love	hate		

APPENDIX ITEM 36

PROVERBS — SYNONYMOUS PARALLELISM

A *proverb* is a short, forceful saying of a useful thought written in expressive language.

In synonymous parallelism the first line states a fact. The second line does the same with different words. The same truth is expressed in very similar terms.

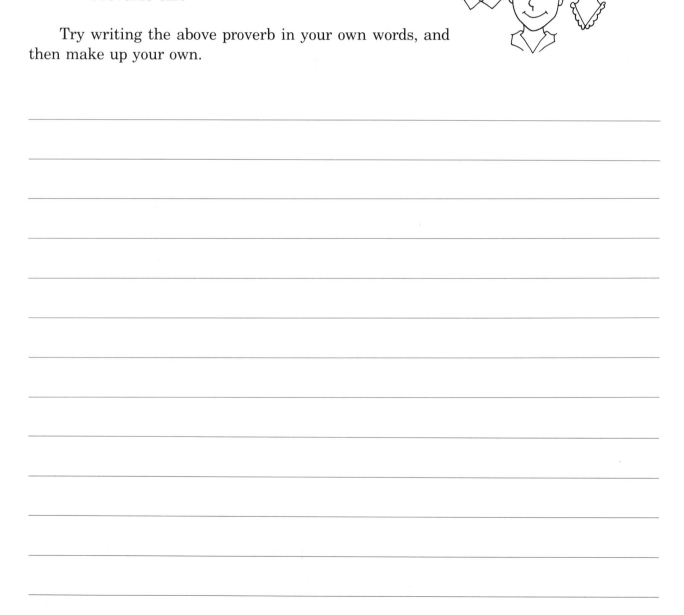

> My son, keep thy father's commandments,
> and forsake not the law of thy mother.
> >   Proverbs 6:20

Try writing the above proverb in your own words, and then make up your own.

From *The Poetry Corner* by Arnold Cheyney © 1982 Scott, Foresman and Company.

APPENDIX ITEM 37

PROVERBS — ANTITHETICAL PARALLELISM

A *proverb* is a short, forceful saying of a useful thought written in expressive language.

In antithetical parallelism the first sentence states a fact or truth and the second sentence gives an opposite view.

    A soft answer turneth away wrath,
    But grievous words stir up anger.
        Proverbs 15:1

Try rewriting the above proverb in your own words and then make up some of your own using the opposites suggested.

_____

_____

past – future; friend – foe; big – little; clean – dirty

_____

_____

_____

_____

_____

_____

APPENDIX ITEM 38

APPROXIMATION POEMS

An *approximation* poem is one that you have probably done already without realizing it. Have you ever started saying, "Roses are red/Violets are blue" . . . and then added your own ending? That is an approximation poem; it is similar to the original.

Try changing some of the Mother Goose rhyming words in italics to your own rhyming words.

There was an old woman who

   lived in a *shoe,*

   _____

She had so many children she didn't

   know what to *do;*

   _____

She gave them some broth without

   any *bread.*

   _____

She whipped them all soundly and put

   them to *bed.*

   _____

Choose your own and try it below.

APPENDIX ITEM 39

RHYMING WORDS

air	dimmer	box	booed	cheer
bear	glimmer	clocks	brewed	clear
care	simmer	docks	chewed	dear
chair	skimmer	flocks	dude	hear
dare	swimmer	fox	food	near
fair	trimmer	knocks	mewed	rear
glare		rocks	stewed	appear
hair	acre	socks		sincere
	baker	mailbox	bug	
ache	shaker	chicken pox	dug	breezy
bake	taker		hug	easy
brake	jailbreaker	brim	jug	freezy
cake	shoemaker	dim	rug	greasy
make	undertaker	grim	shrug	sneezy
snake			snug	
steak	bald	am	thug	dummy
take	called	clam	fireplug	gummy
	hauled	ham	spark plug	mummy
bacon	scald	jam		rummy
shaken	stalled	ram	fickle	scummy
taken	installed	slam	nickle	tummy
awaken		swam	pickle	yummy
mistaken	all	program	tickle	
overtaken	ball			bump
undertaken	call	and	bleed	chump
	crawl	band	deed	clump
bright	fall	brand	need	dump
fight	shawl	hand	seed	hump
height	small	sand	agreed	jump
kite	tall	stand	precede	plump
might		command	centipede	pump
sight	blip	demand		thump
tight	chip		creepy	
write	clip	bed	sleepy	bench
	dip	bread	tepee	clench
billed	drip	dead		French
build	hip	spread		stench
filled	nip	instead		wrench
killed	rip	arrowhead		
thrilled	ship	overfed		
willed	trip			

blind
find
mind
signed
wind

self
shelf
herself
myself
yourself

club
rub
shrub
bathtub
rub-a-dub

bride
cried
died
hide
ride
side
cockeyed
defied
fireside

crumble
fumble
grumble
humble
rumble
stumble
tumble

bell
fell
shell
smell
tell
well
yell

beat
cheat
eat
feet
greet
heat
meat
meet
seat
street
sweet
wheat

bunk
drunk
flunk
skunk
stunk
sunk

blues
brews
choose
cruise
dues
glues
news
snooze

ash
bash
cash
dash
flash
gash
hash
lash
mash
rash
sash
slash
trash

beard
cheered
cleared
neared
sheared
smeared
steered
weird

cease
crease
fleece
geese
grease
Greece
niece
peace
piece

List other rhyming words here.

_____

_____

_____

_____

_____

_____

_____

_____

_____

_____

_____

_____

_____

From *The Poetry Corner* by Arnold Cheyney © 1982 Scott, Foresman and Company.

APPENDIX ITEM 40

COUPLETS

Couplets are two-line poems that match in length and rhyme. Here's one you may remember:

Jumping Jack, jumping Jack,
Missed a crack and broke his back.

Try making your own couplets using these rhyming words. If you want, use other rhyming words.

_____ ash   _____ hide

_____ cash   _____ ride

box – fox   _____

height – kite   _____

bug – hug   _____

tall – small   _____

beat – cheat   _____

bacon – awaken   _____

shake – steak   _____

plump – thump   _____

beard — weird   _____

APPENDIX ITEM 41

TRIPLETS

Triplets are three-line poems that often rhyme. They are sometimes riddles. Do you know this one?

Higher than a house
Higher than a tree;
Oh, whatever can that be?

Try making up your own riddles as triplets. You can rhyme all three lines, the first two only, the last two only, or the first and the last.

From *The Poetry Corner* by Arnold Cheyney © 1982 Scott, Foresman and Company.

APPENDIX ITEM 42

QUATRAINS

The *quatrain* is a four-line poem that has several ways of rhyming last lines. Here is an old favorite:

Peter, Peter, pumpkin *eater,*
    Had a wife and couldn't keep *her,*
He put her in a pumpkin *shell,*
    And there he kept her very *well.*

Try making your own quatrains with these rhyming words. If you need to change any words, do so.

_____ (no rhyme)

_____ chair

_____ (no rhyme)

_____ dare

_____ mewed

_____ stewed

_____ jug

_____ hug

_____ rumble

_____ ride

_____ tumble

_____ cried

APPENDIX ITEM 43

EPITAPHS

An *epitaph* is a saying written on a tombstone in a cemetery. Those who pass by read them and consider what the writer is saying to them. Some are amusing but also make you think about your actions, such as this one:

This is the grave of Mike O'Day
Who died maintaining his right of way.
His right was clear, his will was strong,
But he's just as dead as if he'd been wrong.

Epitaphs can take most any form of poetic writing but they should be short (how much can be written on a tombstone?) and catchy.

APPENDIX ITEM 44

EPIGRAMS

An *epigram* is a short witty thought, sometimes a poem. The ending often has a twist that is amusing or provokes one to think.

Thomas Carlyle wrote an epigram many years ago along this line:

The greatest of faults, I should say, is to be conscious of none.

Try writing some of your own brand of short, witty epigrams.

APPENDIX ITEM 45

LIMERICKS — EDWARD LEAR

Limericks are five-line poems whose first, second, and fifth lines rhyme and whose third and fourth lines rhyme. Edward Lear made them popular many years ago. He wrote wild and crazy ones to the delight of many children. Here's one example:

> There is a young lady, whose nose,
> Continually prospers and grows.
> When it grew out of sight,
> She exclaimed in a fright,
> "Oh, Farewell to the end of my nose."

Try writing some of your own limericks following the rhyme pattern and beat of Edward Lear's limerick. These starting sentences may help you, then you are on your own:

There was a young girl with large feet,

_____

_____

_____

_____

There once was a boy eating bread,

_____

_____

_____

_____

From *The Poetry Corner* by Arnold Cheyney © 1982 Scott, Foresman and Company.

APPENDIX ITEM 46

LIMERICKS

The fifth line of a *limerick* is often written with a humorous twist. As you read this one aloud (listen to the rhyming lines 1, 2, and 5 and 3 and 4) you will catch the humor at the end.

> There was a young lady of Niger
> Who smiled as she rode on the tiger;
>   They returned from the ride,
>   With the lady inside,
> And the smile on the face of the tiger.

Try writing some limericks with a funny twist to the last line. Here are some starting sentences to help you:

There once was a man who could jump,

_____

_____

_____

_____

Across the great sky flew the geese,

_____

_____

_____

APPENDIX ITEM 47

THE GRAND OLD DUKE OF YORK

Medium	The Grand Old Duke of York
	He had ten thousand men,
High	He marched them up a very high hill
Low	And he marched them down again.
High	And when he was up he was up
Low	And when he was down he was down
Medium	And when he was only half way up
	He was neither
High	up
Medium	nor
Low	down.

From *The Poetry Corner* by Arnold Cheyney © 1982 Scott, Foresman and Company.

APPENDIX ITEM 48

THE CHICKENS

From *The Poetry Corner* by Arnold Cheyney © 1982 Scott, Foresman and Company.

All   Said the first little chicken,
      With a queer little squirm,
Solo   "I wish I could find
      A fat little worm!"

All   Said the next little chicken,
      With an odd little shrug:
Solo   "I wish I could find
      A fat little bug!"

All   Said the third little chicken,
      With a sharp little squeal,
Solo   "I wish I could find
      Some nice yellow meal!"

All   Said the fourth little chicken,
      With a small sigh of grief,
Solo   "I wish I could find
      A little green leaf!"

All   Said the fifth little chicken,
      With a faint little moan,
Solo   "I wish I could find
      A wee gravel-stone!"

Solo/all "Now, see here," said the mother,
      From the green garden-patch
Solo   "If you want any breakfast,
      Just come here and scratch."

          –Unknown

APPENDIX ITEM 49

POOR OLD WOMAN

There was an old woman who swallowed a fly.
Oh, my! Swallowed a fly!
Poor old woman, I think she'll die.

There was an old woman who swallowed a spider;
Right down inside her she swallowed a spider;
She swallowed the spider to kill the fly.
Oh, my! Swallowed a fly!
Poor old woman, I think she'll die.

There was an old woman who swallowed a bird.
How absurd to swallow a bird!
She swallowed the bird to kill the spider,
She swallowed the spider to kill the fly.
Oh, my! Swallowed a fly!
Poor old woman, I think she'll die.

There was an old woman who swallowed a cat,
Fancy that! She swallowed a cat!
She swallowed the cat to kill the bird,
She swallowed the bird to kill the spider,
She swallowed the spider to kill the fly.
Oh, my! Swallowed a fly!
Poor old woman, I think she'll die.

There was an old woman who swallowed a dog.
She went the whole hog! She swallowed a dog!
She swallowed the dog to kill the cat,
She swallowed the cat to kill the bird,
She swallowed the bird to kill the spider,
She swallowed the spider to kill the fly.
Oh my! Swallowed a fly!
Poor old woman, I think she'll die.

There was an old woman who swallowed a cow.
I don't know how, but she swallowed a cow.
She swallowed the cow to kill the dog,
She swallowed the dog to kill the cat,
She swallowed the cat to kill the bird,
She swallowed the bird to kill the spider,
She swallowed the spider to kill the fly.
Oh, my! Swallowed a fly!
Poor old woman, I think she'll die.

There was an old woman who swallowed a horse!
She died, of course.

–Unknown

From *The Poetry Corner* by Arnold Cheyney © 1982 Scott, Foresman and Company.

APPENDIX ITEM 50

POETRY BOOK

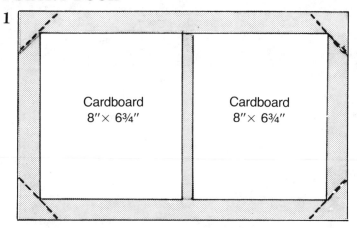

Cut cloth 10″ × 16″. Place cardboard in 1″ from each side. Glue cardboard on the cloth. Cut off corners.

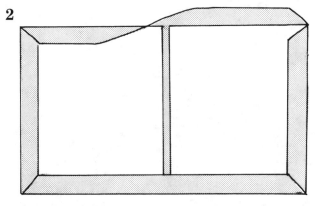

Put glue around edges of cloth and pull them over the cardboard.

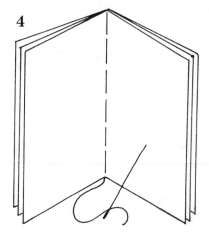

Cut newsprint sheets 14″ × 18″. Sew or staple them in the center.

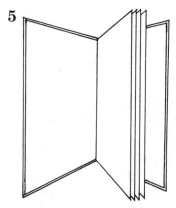

Glue outside sheets of newsprint to the cardboards.